D1603497

Mastering
Product Experience in SaaS

How to Deliver Personalized Product Experiences
with Product-led Go-to-Market Strategy

Nick Bonfiglio • Mickey Alon

aptrinsic

Table of Contents

Opening Thoughts

by Nick Bonfiglio

CEO AND FOUNDER OF APTRINSIC

Building a great product is hard. Getting people to try your product is even harder. But the ultimate challenge is to ensure that customers not only try, but keep using your product over time. Succeed, and you achieve the ultimate goal of growing a base of customers who are loyal to both your product and your brand. Those who continuously derive value from your product will share their experiences with colleagues, peers, and friends; and there's no better marketing than a referral from someone who loves your product.

How do you build products that people love? How do you make it easy and convenient for customers to try and buy your product?

While those challenges are big, one of the largest and perhaps most important challenges to solve is this: understanding your customers' needs and what they value in your products and improving how they experience your product.

No wonder it's only getting more challenging to be a product manager. Today's product managers must take more data, and the overall customer experience, into consideration as they make critical product-related decisions. It is not enough to understand technology, UX, new software development methodologies, and the business side of your customers. Long-term product success requires a deep understanding of, and ability to influence, user behaviors inside your product.

This is especially true for product managers at Software-as-a-Service (SaaS) companies—that is, enterprise software companies. For their companies to stay competitive and grow, they must adopt a new go-to-market strategy, a customer acquisition process, and most importantly, a new way of thinking about the customer experience.

Early in my career, I learned how challenging it is to acquire, engage, and keep users in your product. At 3DO, I helped bring to life one of the very first internet games, Meridian 59—a massively multiplayer online game that made it possible for people from around the world to play together. Our goal, obviously, was to build game features that would keep customers playing for as long as possible. Usually, players are not getting paid to spend hours playing the game, nor do they have a boss urging them to keep playing. So how do you create an environment where people willingly spend a significant amount of their time?

Gaming companies were the first to realize the importance of understanding players' (a.k.a. users') goals and behaviors. They pay more attention to user behaviors than to their demographics. At 3DO, we used the classical player behavioral segmentation—what is now commonly referred to as the Bartle taxonomy of four player types—which focuses on developing features aimed at increasing user playing time and engagement. Players were able to customize their avatars for a more personalized in-game experience. We awarded points for exploring the game world; points were also earned by beating weaker opponents and aggressive creatures. But more importantly, we built in-game e-mail and bulletin boards, guild voting, and political appointments. Even our user support system was built into the game; our support staff had their own avatars, and any player could ask questions and interact with these special support characters while playing the game.

Every feature was designed to keep users playing the game. Every communication with users happened inside the game. You could say that we used our game to acquire, retain, and grow our user base.

The idea of engaging customers through product experiences stayed with me as I moved into the enterprise software world, most recently at a company offering marketing automation as SaaS. While at Marketo, I chaired our Global Product Council, where we faced similar challenges as those at 3DO. Our goal was identifying the right behavioral data, and devising the right adoption methodologies, to drive increased growth without significantly increasing our customer acquisition costs.

But getting accurate and insightful behavioral data at an enterprise software company proved to be more challenging. That's because we lacked a way to capture real-time product usage and customer profile data in a single system. Like most other enterprise companies, we cobbled together disparate systems which provided access to some amount of forensic data at best.

Compounding matters was the reliance on a sales-led go-to-market (GTM) model, as is common in most software companies. In other words, our sales organization took the lead for all sales development, customer meetings, demos, proof-of-concept installations, and the like. During this time, we came to realize that this expensive GTM model wasn't going to work for less expensive SaaS offerings like ours that were disrupting incumbent, on-premise software providers.

Enter the marketing-led GTM model, where sales development representative roles were created to work in conjunction with account executives. This newer model gave companies more favorable prospect-to-sales-representative ratios. It was tilted toward mass lead generation and quick turnaround, leveraging the internet for webinars and online demos, while reducing office visits to far-flung prospect sites. But even this didn't prove enough to address our needs and goals to help us get the insights we needed.

During my time at Marketo, I remember a meeting where people were guessing about issues with our newly introduced products. Because we had no first-hand data about how our customers were using our products, we couldn't make informed business decisions. Further, our cross-functional team didn't have the capability or tools to influence a customer's adoption journey while they were using our products. However—and here's the frustrating part for any product person—everyone seemed to have an opinion on what to change or add to the product.

We realized that software product teams needed a better way to drive and measure adoption, influence user behavior, and optimize in-product customer experiences. My experience in the gaming industry proved to be vital to understanding what enterprise software companies are finally starting to realize: The customer experience and behaviors in your product should inform how you drive your GTM strategy.

The need to shift SaaS companies to a product-led GTM strategy became apparent. As a global product team, we worked hard at Marketo to innovate and create great products. However, without effective customer adoption strategies to drive new growth and upsell our existing base, we might as well have left those products on the proverbial internet shelf. It was a disappointing reality check, and it was at that point that the market opportunity became very evident to Mickey and me—so we decided to do something about it.

We wrote this book to share empirical data about what has been happening to make this new product-led GTM strategy the preferred model for SaaS teams and companies undergoing digital transformation. It provides practical ideas for how to turn your software product into a personalized customer experience, and a go-to-market machine that will create more value for your customers and company. We also envision a new organizational culture emerging, geared toward generating Product-Qualified Leads (PQLs) rather than Marketing-Qualified Leads (MQLs). It is a customer-oriented culture that will fuel the next evolution of GTM strategies, and move us away from mass-lead demand generation toward creating and curating customer experiences.

As a CEO, I well understand the importance of identifying the key levers the company leader can pull to make the greatest impact on their business; and I am convinced that a product-led GTM strategy is the one lever every SaaS company needs to pull in order to make their businesses lasting ones.

by Mickey Alon

CPO AND CO-FOUNDER OF APTRINSIC

The nature of SaaS startups requires founders to pay attention to product adoptions and renewals as soon as the company hits a certain level of initial growth. In the early days of Insightera, all my co-founder, Mike Telem, and I cared about was closing the next deal. Getting prospective customers to agree with the premise behind our product wasn't difficult; delivering meaningful personalized website experiences to each individual visitor would help B2B companies increase conversion rates. But building a new and innovative product with well-defined requirements, on time and on budget, did not guarantee success.

We were operating with scarce resources in a highly competitive market. We had to quickly discover the path to building a sustainable business, and that meant testing our hypothesis early with minimal investment so we could validate which parts of our strategy were working and which ones were failing.

Measuring adoption, getting real feedback, and validating our assumptions was not a simple task as we passed 30 paying customers. In the process of getting these accounts to adopt our product and realize its full value, we discovered interesting patterns that separated early adopters from our early majority.

We continued experimenting with new features that were part of an annual roadmap strategy. Getting feedback and re-prioritizing our roadmap based on real value discovery was very resource-intensive and complicated. We wanted to decommission features that were not adopted over time and didn't fit our product strategy any more, but it was challenging to reach consensus around these decisions since we didn't have enough data about which customers were using which features and the revenue impact of pulling a given feature from them. Yet avoiding those decisions has immediate and long-term impact on delivering the right product to the market!

Along the way, we pinpointed our ideal account size and the sequence of core features that, once adopted, would lead to successful adoption and renewal (we called those "Golden Features"). Our goal was now to influence user behavior and guide customers to use these Golden Features through our webinars and e-mail marketing campaigns, but those marketing tools were ineffective—mainly because the timing didn't match the context of what our users were doing with our product. In other words, Tuesday at 10 a.m., or a day of the week determined by the most recent e-mail open-rate study, in no way correlated to our customers' actual product usage. The right time was when they were using the product and needed to get something done; that was when they were most receptive to our messaging.

We started tracking our own app so we could engage our users more contextually, based on their stage in the customer lifecycle and use case. In essence, we were following the same idea as that encompassed in our product: If you provide the right content to the right prospect in real time, based on intent and actual behavior, you're more likely to win their undivided attention.

As we grew our customer base to 60 paying customers and signed on some hot logos, we knew we had a product/market fit. My focus as CEO shifted from proving our business model to driving business growth. I soon realized that using a traditional outbound B2B sales model wouldn't move the needle fast enough. Rather, we needed to adopt a different, more scalable model to win against larger and more established brands.

We found that offering product demos and trials worked much better than a long sales process or outbound nurturing. That approach made it possible to clearly demonstrate our product's value, and differentiate ourselves from the competitors, whose sales forces were armed with slideware and buzzwords. Showing the product was worth a thousand slides, especially when we could demonstrate a relevant use case as part of a quick feature walk-through.

Thanks to the rapid changes in our digital space—both in technology and in customer expectations—we were able to launch our product, drive awareness, and become the leading B2B real-time website personalization player. In less than two years, we went from receiving our seed funding to being acquired by Marketo, the fastest growing leader in the marketing automation space. We were fortunate to join this iconic company, which was built by the founders from the ground up and had a highly committed product leadership team.

Once we became part of Marketo, we had a big a-ha! moment. Although Marketo was a multi-billion-dollar company, it faced the same challenges as any startup. It needed to figure out how to:

- Get validated metrics about current product usage compared with customer lifetime value (CLV)
- Drive strategic product decisions based on empirical facts
- Tie bookings and revenue to engineering resources
- Increase adoption to newly launched products, set measurable goals, and take effective actions to improve bottom line results

That realization led to the founding of Aptrinsic, and in this book, we share what we each have learned along the way about what it takes to succeed with a SaaS company. We explain how to deliver a winning customer-centric experience strategy to your customers throughout the customer lifecycle, from acquisition to up-sell/X-sell. We show how to implement a faster and more effective product-led GTM strategy to meet changing customer expectations, and how to optimize CAC and increase CLV by building better contextual relationships through personalized product-driven engagement.

As a seasoned product professional and SaaS executive, I'm incredibly excited by the way a product-led GTM strategy can change the game for SaaS companies. We're already seeing its impact on Aptrinsic, and are confident it can change the future of many other companies for the better. Here's to your product-led success!

Part I

The Importance of Customer Experience

"You have to start with customer experience and work back toward the technology—not the other way around."

STEVE JOBS

Chapter 1
Welcome to the Customer Experience Era

Any sophisticated product manager will tell you their product is only a success when their customers succeed by using it. Rightfully, they feel frustrated by lackluster adoption or usage of the amazing product they delivered to market. In many companies, such failures are pinned on a certain group or even an individual; but in the era of the customer, everyone across the organization is responsible for product success. It all hinges on putting customer experience front and center.

Customer experience has become critical for all companies in the experience economy[1]. To be competitive, or even to survive, every organization will have to become a customer experience business. In fact, a study published in the Harvard Business Review[2] found that customers who had the best experiences with a transaction-based business spent 140 percent more than customers who had the worst experiences. And the experience matters just as much for subscription-based businesses: The same study revealed that customers who had the best experiences as subscribers were 74 percent more likely to be subscribers one year later. On the other hand, customers who had the worst experiences were only 43 percent likely to be subscribers a year later.

Consumer companies were the first to respond to changing customer expectations—think Amazon, Netflix, Uber, and Airbnb. In many ways, our experience with these brands is about far more than what we are buying from them; it's also about the experience of buying from them.

This trend spills over into B2B and enterprise software markets, and results in what is often called a consumerization of enterprise software. If you can purchase a consumer product or service without interacting with a representative, then why must you go through a complicated purchase process? Why should you need to submit a lead form to try a software product? It's getting harder for enterprise software companies to justify the need for a complex buying process in a world where frictionless customer experiences are on the rise; and that experience now starts the moment a potential customer becomes aware of a company or its product, and extends to the actual point of purchase and beyond.

Rather than being intimidated by the way that digital disruptors like Uber and others have upended entire industries, or brushing them off as irrelevant, forward-thinking industry stalwarts and SaaS pioneers are thinking strategically. They are eager to learn from these trailblazers, and find a way to reinvent their business models and catch up in a world increasingly shaped by consumer experiences.

Though the SaaS business model was revolutionary and promised a truly modern user experience, few companies have yet cracked the code on how to enable the frictionless end-to-end experience that today's customers crave. Those that do will be rewarded in the form of increasingly higher rates of conversion, retention, and loyalty.

Enter digital transformation, which empowers organizations to completely reimagine how they interact with prospects and customers as they are using products. In other words, it puts them in the highly coveted position of understanding and engaging with prospects and customers in product, essentially transforming their approach to focus on the product as an experience.

More on this later, though. First, let's dig a bit more into the impact of digital transformation across industries.

1.1. Digital Transformation is Changing Everything

Between 2000 and 2014, 52 percent of Fortune 500 companies disappeared,[3] either by going bankrupt or through acquisition. We will look at how digital transformation created big winners and losers for those selling retail books, providing movie rentals, offering recruiting services, and participating in the hospitality business. The winners adapted and worked with the changes brought by digital transformation, while those who didn't adapt languished.

> **Digital transformation** is the change associated with the application of digital technology to all aspects of human society[4]

Retail Books: Borders vs. Amazon

Before the internet gained mass appeal, Borders' competitive advantage was to offer the biggest selection of books in stores. However, new technology allowed internet companies to offer practically every book in print in the world, without the overhead costs associated with prime real estate. Jeff Bezos of Amazon envisioned the importance of this digital transformation early on, and created a new customer experience—and the largest internet-based retailer in the world.

Now we expect to find any book (and much more) on Amazon within seconds, order it with a couple of clicks, and receive it tomorrow—or even instantly on your Kindle or iPad. Amazon leveraged digital transformation to provide a great online experience that has now extended to nearly every conceivable product in the world. Meanwhile, Borders Groups sank from a $3.2 billion-revenue business in 2000 to one filing for bankruptcy in 2011[5].

Movie Rentals: Blockbuster vs. Netflix

Netflix embraced digital transformation and designed new customer experiences that raised their expectations. Customers no longer had to drive to a local store to rent a DVD; they could order it online, receive it at their doorstep, and never pay a late fee again.

That was revolutionary. In 2000, Blockbuster made almost $800 million in late fees (roughly 16 percent of its revenue[6]). Reed Hastings, the founder of Netflix, understood that late fees only make customers resent your brand, not become loyal to it. The same year, Blockbuster considered but ultimately passed on purchasing Netflix for $50 million[7] at a time when Blockbuster was generating more than $4.9 billion in revenue[8]. It was a short-sighted, fateful choice: in 2013, Blockbuster closed its doors, and Netflix became a ubiquitous media company, with $4.4 billion in revenue[9].

Furthermore, Netflix was able to transition when the next wave of digital innovation crashed into the media industry. When high-speed broadband internet became available to a larger segment of the population, Netflix launched video streaming, which further improved customer experiences. The Netflix story provides a good lesson: Your primary revenue stream today may not be the primary stream tomorrow[10].

Recruiting: Monster vs. LinkedIn

Remember Monster.com, the original online job board? It was one of the first big successes of the internet in the late 1990s and early 2000s. In 2006, Monster had a market capitalization of $7.5 billion, but just a decade later, the company was acquired for much, much less: $429 million[11].

Monster made a grave miscalculation: it failed to recognize the importance of social networks when it came to job searches. Professional networks allow you not just to expand your connections and showcase your work, but also to empower companies to recruit large pools of candidates who are passively looking for new opportunities. That's what LinkedIn realized, completely changing how people interact within professional networks; and the recruiting industry had to adapt as a result.

We've seen the kicker to this story before: Monster declined to buy LinkedIn during its early days. LinkedIn, with its innovative recruitment products, ended up eating Monster's revenues.

Hospitality: Airbnb vs. Hotels

Airbnb, an online marketplace for people to list, discover, and book private residences around the world, is a more recent example of a company that understands how digital transformation provides a tremendous opportunity to build a better customer experience. While Airbnb owns no real estate, it has become a powerful player in the global hospitality sector, taking on established hotel chains. Airbnb has more than 3 million listings worldwide, compared to Marriott, which, after its recent merger with Starwood, has just 1.2 million rooms[12]. While a hotel room is different in many ways from a private apartment, Airbnb has driven many travelers out of traditional hotels, all due to its unique business model—which became possible thanks to digital transformation. Staying in a quaint neighborhood creates a unique traveling experience that can't be replicated by traditional, standardized hotels, in which there typically is little different about the experience in Rome than in Bangkok. Certainly Airbnb had to implement a complex security and reviews system in order to assure users they were safe staying in private homes--a process hotels can skip—yet they've done so largely successfully.

The fact that Airbnb is a platform, and owns no real estate other than its own headquarters, minimizes its costs and increases its profit margins. These savings can then be transferred to consumers—and Wall Street likes the model. Within just nine years, the industry disruptor has been valued at $31 billion—just nine billion shy of Marriott, which has been in business since 1927[13]. The rise of Airbnb has forced traditional hotel chains to focus more on their core customers—business travelers—while Airbnb provides greater flexibility and a more authentic experience for leisure travelers. With Airbnb[14], it's not just about a place to stay; it's about having a unique offline experience[15] in an unfamiliar city.

So what happened to Borders, Blockbuster, Monster, and the hotel chains? How is it possible to go from billions in revenue to bankrupt in as little as a decade? Simply put, these once-stellar companies failed to recognize the early wave of digital transformation from the physical to the digital world. Borders and Blockbuster stuck to old business models; Monster failed to adapt its product and business model to address changes in how people communicate professionally and search for jobs; and Airbnb is outperforming established hotel chains by using digital transformation to provide unique experiences.

Digital transformation reaches all aspects of human society, and will continue to influence software creation and delivery. As Marc Andreessen famously said, "Software is eating the world[16]," meaning every company will become a software company, engaging with its customers through digital channels. Even a dry cleaner can build a loyal customer base by sending a real-time notification when your order is ready. Hair salons can build a way for customers to easily schedule appointments via mobile. As the technology itself becomes cheap and commoditized, it's the experiences you provide to customers that create a competitive advantage.

Borders, Blockbuster, and Monster failed to fully recognize that digital transfor-mation creates a new, more efficient, and effective way to engage with customers.

1.2 Customer Expectations are Constantly Evolving

Digital transformation also brought a whole new wave of online-first and digital-only services.

eSurance is one of the first companies to bring car insurance online; why would you, as a customer, waste your time driving to a local insurance store, or even talking to a representative over the phone, when you can answer a few questions online and get insured within 10 minutes? Why spend time writing and mailing a check, when you can pay your monthly fee via a mobile app? Why wait on the phone to speak to a representative when you can send a quick message?

eSurance harnessed digital transformation to create a better experience for customers while also building a competitive advantage over traditional insurance companies. There is no need for local offices, since most of the transactions can be processed electronically, and eSurance doesn't need a large team of representatives and salespeople. This results in significant cost savings; quicker and more convenient purchases result in customer happiness.

Revolutionary consumer companies reimagined how stellar experiences could provide enormous value to customers. In cases like Apple, Uber, Lyft, Amazon, and Airbnb, this changed entire industries, or invented a new category of products and services. These disruptors have raised the bar of customer expectations; now the enterprise software industry must catch up.

Bill Price, President of Driva Solutions and author of "Your Customer Rules![17]," points out that as an engineer or procurement manager is buying software, he or she is exposed to multiple customer experiences. All of these set the standard for expectations[18]. The line between customer expectations for B2C and B2B is blurring. Customer needs in today's economy are based, first of all, on knowing your customers and remembering your relationship with them. Customers want you to supply choices and make the decision and process easy. They expect you to trust, value, and surprise them. Most of all, you need to help your customers be better and do more.

1.3 The Third Wave of SaaS: The Customer Experience Era

When we buy and consume great products and services, and experience brands in our daily lives, we may question why enterprise software products and services do not match our expectations. This shift can be attributed to two very simple ideas: We're all more active "shoppers," and the web and technological innovations have removed friction from traditional business processes.

The early days of digital transformation brought a new subscription-based business model to enterprise software. Today, SaaS is synonymous with B2B and enterprise software. SaaS opened the door to many other variations of a subscription-based model in the B2B market, such as Infrastructure-as-a-Service (IaaS) and Data-as-a-Service (DaaS), to name just two. To succeed in an Everything-as-a-Service world—the new ideal—companies must fundamentally change how they think about customer experience and engagement. It requires creating experiences, engagements, journeys, and touchpoints to match and exceed customer expectations.

Digital transformation has brought all businesses online, so even though SaaS businesses were already digital and service-based, they now need to join the third wave—customer experience—to keep up.

The first wave of SaaS replaced on-premises software installations, introducing many advantages by moving to the cloud. The second wave brought major changes in workflow and processes. It's the third wave, however—with its focus on customer experience and personalization—that has revolutionized how companies go to market. See Table 1.1 for details.

No matter where your company started, it must be able to deliver a unique and consistent experience across every channel. Offering extra features is no longer enough to make you competitive.

Table 1.1 - The Evolution of the SaaS Industry

SaaS 1.0	SaaS 2.0	SaaS 3.0
Replaced on-premise	**Introduced solutions streamlined on processes and workflows**	**Focuses on customer experience**
• Moved the system of record from on-premise to the cloud • Introduced no major new functionality, changes in processes, or workflows • Provided flexible pricing with subscription model	• Provided additional value to system of record • Delivered new functionality and integration with system of record via API • Proved more affordable and accessible	• Differentiates primarily via personalized customer experiences • Personalizes customer experience with product, pricing, message, engagement, and channels • Delivers omnichannel customer experience

First wave: from on-premise to the cloud

Salesforce pioneered and popularized the SaaS model for enterprise software. In the early SaaS 1.0 wave, cloud solutions emerged as the replacements for on-premise solutions, which involved purchasing and installing expensive servers and software and enduring a drawn-out onboarding process. This shift to the cloud provided a tremendous value-add for companies.

Early SaaS products were often less expensive and more convenient than traditional client-server options. The SaaS revolution lowered entry cost, and provided flexible pricing with a subscription model. Negotiating a multi-year contract with a vendor became a thing of the past. Buyers no longer had to make the risky and often irreversible decision to buy on-premise software that their company would be stuck with for years to come. Moreover, SaaS companies made obsolete the switching costs when an organization invests enormous resources on hardware, support, and employee training.

Second wave: new processes and workflows plus affordability

SaaS companies in the second wave (the SaaS 2.0 era) brought more features to customers at a lower cost. These new SaaS solutions helped companies evaluate their current processes and tactics to find more efficient ways of solving business problems. In an essay, Tomasz Tunguz, venture partner at Redpoint, called SaaS 1.0 companies the "displacers", and SaaS 2.0 companies the "disruptors."[19] He points out that the shift from SaaS 1.0 to 2.0 moved from a system of record to workflow solutions. Earlier systems of record we associate with the SaaS 1.0 era provided a single source of truth about a particular department. Workflow solutions, associated with the SaaS 2.0 era, allowed companies to change and improve organization-wide processes that enabled them to achieve higher efficiencies and effectiveness.

Third wave: customer experience and personalization

The third wave will turn SaaS products into online services, and will be based on interactions with software rather than with people. This changes how people try, buy, and use software.

Buying used to be a more predictable and linear process, requiring direct interaction between buyers and sales teams. But the buying process has dramatically changed. Customers now research, evaluate, select, and share experiences that feel more like consumer experiences, involving numerous interactions across multiple touchpoints.

Thanks to digital transformation, buyers can access more product-related and thought leadership content through a variety of channels and devices, including the web, mobile, wearables, social media, and online customer reviews. This leads to more self-directed customer journeys during the buying process. According to Forrester Research, two-thirds to 90 percent of the buyer's journey[20] is completed prior to engaging a salesperson. The challenge is to effectively manage customer experiences and journeys for a contemporary buying process.

Competing with features and pricing is no longer an effective strategy for SaaS companies. Competitors can match your prices and copy your product features and marketing messages. But unique customer experiences aren't easily duplicated. Today, you need to be part of the third wave of SaaS. As Steve Jobs said, rather than focus first on the product or service, start with the customer experience you want to deliver; then figure out what combination of product features, pricing, and messages will enable you to deliver that experience.

Some companies, such as Salesforce, began in the first wave of SaaS and have successfully evolved through the second and third waves. Others, such as Marketo, Hubspot, and Apttus, started out as second-wave companies and must move forward. Some newer companies built a competitive advantage by focusing on customer experience as one of their core differentiators. The third-wave companies include Slack, Invision, Asana, and Zoom.us.

Zoom.us, a video conferencing service, is an interesting example. Dozens of videoconferencing solutions were available before Zoom was launched in 2011. However, in just two years, Zoom grew[21] its customer base from 4,000 to 65,000 organizations, and expanded its reach from 3 million to 40 million individuals. It was able to do so by focusing on how customers experience their product. For instance, Zoom made it easy to try its service, and simplified the payment process. Other examples of successful enterprise software companies that create a competitive advantage around customer experience include Slack, Asana, Dropbox, and InVision.

What do all of these companies have in common? All are focusing on driving prospects to their product earlier in the buying cycle. Slack, Asana, Dropbox, InVision, and Zoom.us do not ask prospects to submit lead forms. Instead, they invite them to try and to experience the product themselves. They are engaging customers by leading with their products.

Digital transformation changes how customers research, buy, and experience products and services. It closes the gap between B2B and B2C experiences, in what can now be called more human-to-human interactions[22]. The buying process in business markets now resembles the buying process in consumer markets. An increase in communication tools including social media, and interactive work environments such as conferencing and chat, has changed thr expectations of buyers worldwide. Today, the buying process in business environments has become more social, more real-time, and more cross-functional, with more influencers involved from across the company. McKinsey research[23] shows that, on average, "a B2B customer will regularly use six different interaction channels throughout the decision journey, and almost 65 percent will come away from it frustrated by inconsistent experiences" across these channels.

Three waves of SaaS have moved software companies into the cloud, changed processes and workflows, and now, focused on customer experience. SaaS has been consumerized, which means that customers now expect to try the product early in a buying cycle. The good news is that this gives companies a way to measure customer activity, and fine-tune how they market and sell their products. As we explain in detail further in the book, getting prospects to try software early via free trials or free versions of the product (i.e., freemium) creates more and better opportunities to engage customers.

Ask yourself this question: Why would a prospective customer jump through hoops to get a glimpse of your product? Simply put, fewer people will once they are exposed to free trials and freemium.

Before we leap into how companies should approach customer experience, and what strategies enable them to build close relationships with customers, let's define customer experience.

Chapter 2
Defining Customer Experience

As we have seen, digital transformation makes it possible for companies to reimagine customer experience. Many industries have been disrupted by a new wave of companies that redesigned customer experience through the whole value delivery chain. Think of Uber and Airbnb as perfect examples of consumer companies that completely redesigned customer experience in their industries, and raised the bar for customer expectation across the board. This trend has now shifted to the SaaS industry, where differentiation on features and pricing is no longer enough to be competitive. Customer experience becomes the key priority regardless of the organization's guiding principles, culture, size, or budget.

So far, we've used the term customer experience without defining what we mean by it. In recent years, it has become a common term. But as with other concepts and ideas that seem obvious, we face the danger of misunderstanding if we don't define precisely what we mean by customer experience.

2.1 What Are Customer Experience, Touchpoints, Interactions, and Engagements?

When most people talk about customer experience, they think about customer service, customer satisfaction, customer success, and customer engagement or interaction. It's logical and makes perfect sense, but this is a narrow view. Customer experience is all of the above plus more—much more. It's the totality of all touchpoints, interactions, and engagements with a company or brand.

Think about the last time you bought a product or service, whether it was through Netflix or Pandora's subscription services, a book on Amazon, or SaaS. You likely remember vividly how the whole experience felt. You came into the buying process with certain expectations. The company either fulfilled this expectation, leading to positive emotions and customer experience, or underperformed, making you feel frustrated or angry.

The quality of the customer experience is evaluated based on the perception of how well the company satisfies expectations. Many companies focus on customer satisfaction and customer service. That's good, but let's not forget that if customer expectations are very high, even a great performance can fall short; and in most companies, marketing and sales set those expectations, as these groups are the ones interacting with prospective customers before those buyers experience the product.

With this idea in mind, we define customer experience as follows:

> **Customer experience (CX)** is a customer's perception about a company, brand, or product, based on all touchpoints, interactions, and engagements.

This definition is aligned with how Forrester explains customer experience . Harley Manning, VP of Research at Forrester, asserts that customer experience is the perception of a customer that is based on all interactions between a customer and a company. While we agree with this view, we believe that customer experience is also shaped by word of mouth, ad impressions, and exposure to other corporate messages. Even if these do not necessarily lead to interactions, over time, exposure to a consistent message forms an expectation before a customer ever interacts with a company.

Experiences, as with perceptions, exist only in the mind of an individual who has been engaged on an emotional, physical, and mental level. Therefore, customer experience can't be identical for any two individuals. It's inherently a balanced relationship between what each customer expects, and what he or she gets.

This is why customer experience should include a whole universe of touchpoints, interactions, and engagement that a customer has with a company, brand, or product. This includes everything from conversations with your customer success team to newsletter e-mails, and even to how diverse and open your organization is as a public entity.

Naturally, the question surfaces: what do you mean by touchpoints, interactions, and engagement? "Touchpoint" is sometimes defined as an interaction, and "customer interaction" is often used interchangeably with "customer engagement."

Let's sort this out with an example. While driving on a highway, you notice a large billboard with a clever ad. Regardless of whether you formed any opinion about it or not, the message has registered, either in your conscious or subconscious mind. Is this an interaction? Hardly, since interaction is defined as reciprocal action between two or more parties; but you were exposed to a billboard ad in a passive way. This exposure is what can be best described as a "touchpoint."

Touchpoint (customer touchpoint) is a single moment when a customer comes in contact with, or is exposed to, a company's brand, product, employees, or message through any channel or device.

Customer touchpoints can take place online or offline, as we see with the billboard example. In the SaaS industry, the majority of touchpoints happen through digital channels, but even with extreme digitalization, we can't completely avoid touchpoints in the real world.

Now let's say you walk into a store, and notice a Nike shoe. That's a touchpoint. When you pick up a shoe to feel the texture, or try it on, that's an interaction. In a sense, interaction is a two-way "communication" that happens between a prospective customer and the company or product. (Note that this "communication" can be in the form of the product "transmitting" information, such as the shoe's texture.)

Customer interaction is a two-way communication between a customer and a company's brand or product.

The confusion arises when you think about how interaction is different from engagement. Customer engagement is another widely used term that is losing meaning, because businesses attribute a wide range of customer interactions and touchpoints to customer engagement. We believe customer engagement requires a stricter definition.

Let's define what we mean by exploring the use of engagement in other contexts. Think about the traditional definition of "engagement"—a formal agreement to get married. In this case, engagement is commitment to action. Similarly, "rules of engagement" in the military are the directives that define the circumstances under which action or use of force may be applied. Here, too, "engagement" is a commitment to act, or to characterize the action itself.

Customer engagement is a commitment or agreement of a customer to act.

Other than long-term customer loyalty, the buying event is the ultimate customer engagement.

Let's look at a few examples of touchpoints, interactions, and engagements for a SaaS company.

Table 2.1 - Touchpoint, Interaction, and Engagement Examples in SaaS

Touchpoints	
Definition	**Examples**
Exposure	• Seeing a digital or print ad • Noticing a company's social media post in the feed • Recognizing a corporate logo at a conference • Reading press releases, annual reports, or blogs • Receiving and opening e-mail
Interactions	
Two-way communication	• Commenting on a company's social media post • Messaging with a company's customer support • Chatting with an employee at an industry conference • Sharing an article or social media post • Visiting a website
Engagements	
Commitment or agreement to act	• Signing up for a free trial or freemium • Signing up to attend a webinar • Agreeing to a call with a sales rep • Buying a product or service

We recognize that CUSTOMER INTERACTIONS and CUSTOMER ENGAGEMENT are often used in the industry to mean the same thing, and while we provide a strict definition for each term in this book and believe the difference is significant, to accommodate industry acceptance of the terms being interchangeable, we will treat them as such.

So, in this book, we use "customer engagement" and "interaction" interchangeably.

To summarize, in order to evaluate and shape the customer experience, organi-zations must understand how customer perceptions change across touchpoints and how customers engage with their brand and product.

2.2 Evaluating a Customer Experience Strategy

Your company not only sells products or services, but also delivers customer experience. Every company does, whether as deliberately designed experiences or as a by-product of current processes, strategy, product delivery methods, employee training, and other factors. Even if your company has not defined a customer experience strategy, you are still delivering some kind of experience to customers. A person who is unaware of a law may not escape the liability for violating it; likewise, a company that is not aware of the customer experience it delivers may not escape the consequences.

It is true that companies can't fully control how customers perceive the experience. However, it would be a mistake to use this as an excuse and not evaluate and design experience for your customers—just like your inability to control the odds in poker doesn't mean you should forget about strategy altogether. Lack of a strategy reduces your company's chances of improving customer experiences in any meaningful way. Conversely, actively designing and constantly evaluating the customer experience will significantly improve your odds of delivering great ones. Even non-digital natives and longstanding businesses are "fighting back" by focusing on customer experience. Note Hilton's approach to the customer experience[2] and survey to make sure they're delivering on it[3].

That said, organizations face certain challenges when designing a customer experience strategy.

First, as stated earlier, even an ideal strategy doesn't enable your company to be in full control of the customer experience. How customers perceive your company and what they expect can be based on individual biases, among other things.

Second, despite customers bringing their expectations from consumer products into their interactions with SaaS companies, the customer experience in B2B industry is still quite different. More complex products, longer sales cycles, and multiple stakeholders in buying decisions contribute to the complexity of overseeing how customers feel and think about a company. For example, the IT department could heavily influence the decision to buy a customer relationship management (CRM) system, even though the sales organization is the primary user and decision-maker.

Third, while focusing on individual touchpoints and interactions is important, customer experience has to be evaluated from end to end, through the complete customer lifecycle. Otherwise, a company runs the risk of designing individual interactions that feel disjointed, rather than designing and delivering a holistic experience.

The fourth challenge is that most organizations see customer experience through the lens of a specific part of the business, such as a department (e.g., billing, sales, or customer support). If your company doesn't understand the experience throughout the entire customer lifecycle, and only focuses on touchpoints and interactions driven by specific departments, it will miss important insights.

For example, customers often want to interact less frequently with companies during the buying process. One way to satisfy this would be for organizations to eliminate superfluous steps in the process, but to confidently determine which steps could be removed, you would need to evaluate the entire buying process. That is challenging when the end-to-end process is really a series of patched-together steps handled by different departments.

Even the experience with support is part of the overall equation. Buyers can have a positive interaction with your marketing team and the content they provide; yet seeing the whole journey might help you eliminate some parts of this interaction completely. Just as importantly, a single department or team can only advance the customer experience so far.

Customer experience is not a department in the company. Rather, it's a set of values and processes that spans the entire organization, and enables companies to keep customers at the center of everything they do. Successful companies think about customer experience as corporate, top-level strategy that impacts every part of the business.

> **Customer experience strategy** is an ongoing process of assessing and managing customer experiences across the customer lifecycle.

Since customer experience revolves around a holistic view of all touchpoints and interactions, companies have to design journeys for multiple stakeholders and decision makers. The first step in customer experience strategy is to understand your target organization and buying personas. Then you need to map customer journeys, critical touchpoints, and interactions along the customer lifecycle for each persona in each target organization.

Among the challenges already highlighted, putting yourself in the shoes of a buying organization is hard. Consumers are different from one another in many ways, but understanding the complexities of the B2B buying process is even more challenging. Simply put, you are dealing with more unknowns when analyzing the experience from the standpoint of a buying organization. It is easier for us to relate to individual consumers than to organizations.

2.3 Why is Customer Experience Critical for SaaS Companies?

The SaaS and enterprise software market has become very competitive. It's increasingly difficult to compete on features and pricing alone. Consider how the marketing technology (MarTech) market alone grew from roughly 150 companies in 2011 to over 5,000 unique companies just six years later in 2017[4]. That's 32 times the increase in just six years! If you have a unique technology that can't be replicated or replaced by competitors, good for you. But most companies find themselves up against rivals offering comparable products at similar prices. Providing a unique customer experience is an opportunity to stand out and build strong relationships with customers.

The first major reason why customer experience is critical in today's world is the fact that 30 percent of customers are willing to share bad experiences[5]. Secondly, 19 percent of customers will not trust a company again after just one bad experience[6]. We believe companies are at risk of going out of business if they can't differentiate themselves by creating meaningful customer experiences.

As many successful SaaS companies, such as Slack, Dropbox, InVision, and Zoom.us, realized, customer experience provides a tremendous opportunity to differentiate yourself from competitors and increase growth rates.

Customer experience as a competitive advantage

No two companies can provide identical customer experiences. Your unique customer experiences are rooted in your culture, processes, and policies, and are manifested in every interaction that your customers have with your company and product. Customer experience is a competitive differentiator that's almost impossible to copy. It's the result of your overall corporate strategy and alignment across functions. In other words, it can't be created or delivered by any one department alone.

Threats are no longer coming exclusively from the competition. We're now in an environment where a blog post by an industry influencer can trigger customers to switch in minutes from one SaaS product to another.

Today's connected customers expect a lot from brands, and are loyal when they consume quality products and experiences. Unfortunately, it's easy for companies to deliver poor experiences and value. In turn, they are unable to prevent customers from switching to a competitor that appears to provide a better alternative.

Case in point: According to data in the 2015 Econsultancy and IBM report "**THE CONSUMER CONVERSATION**", either the product or the experience could cause a customer to switch to another provider. When asked about their reason for switching companies, 51 percent of respondents left a company due to experience, while 42 percent switched to a new company based on the belief there was a better product available.

A pleasant customer experience can deliver extra value for customers and strengthen your relationship with them. Customer experience is your company's DNA: a combination of brand, marketing messages, product offering, pricing strategy, processes, policies, and vision.

Customer experience as a growth engine

The long-term economic success of any SaaS company is based on its ability to optimize Customer Acquisition Cost (CAC) and Customer Lifetime Value (CLV). In simple terms, a company needs to make more money from a customer over the lifetime of the relationship than it spent on winning her over. How can subscription-based companies become more profitable at a faster rate by increasing the difference between CLV and CAC?

It starts with the experience of a buyer. A study by Forrester has shown that B2B buyers prefer to self-educate, rather than talk to a sales representative to learn about a product, by a factor of three to one.

With more customers preferring a self-service option, companies can improve customer experience and increase profitability by providing options to try a product early in the buying process. Free trials and freemiums are great at showing the value of a product and bringing prospects to their first "a-ha!" moment. When done right, this strategy can not only improve the customer experience, but also shorten the sales cycle and reduce CACs.

Keeping customers longer and preventing churn will significantly increase revenue growth rate. Customer experience is a great predictor of customer churn rate.

Proactively assessing customer experience enables companies to reduce costs that are the result of a poorly designed customer journey. Eliminating touchpoints and interactions that aren't necessary to evaluate a product or complete the purchase, such as by offering a self-serve way to experience the product up front, is one way to reduce the CAC.

A critical step for SaaS companies is to move prospects from free trials to becoming customers. At this stage, companies can engage them with more personalized experiences based on in-product behavior. Examples include relevant onboarding experiences tailored to the user's role, and what that person is trying to accomplish with the product. Another example is a follow-up e-mail that encourages prospects to continue with the trial they started, but then abandoned.

Free trials and signups that are personalized for customers directly impact CAC and reduce the odds of inactivity or churn early in the customer lifecycle.

> How much is an increase of, for example, 3 percent from trial to customer conversion worth to your organization?

The benefits of personalized customer experiences based on behavioral data do not end when prospects convert. As prospects become customers, organizations need to ensure that the product is delivering value to them on a regular basis, and behavioral data can show early signs of trouble in context as well as with more predictability. Lifetime value can only be sustained if customers continue to derive value from using the product. One way companies can help ensure customers experience value over time is to send an e-mail to a user who has not logged in for over a week, or who is clearly using the product less than in the past.

> Does your team proactively track customer segments with declining usage?

> Do you have built-in mechanisms to re-engage inactive customers in intelligent ways?

When organizations deliver personalized customer experiences, they receive invaluable, continuous feedback on how product features and updates affect customers during specific periods, and can identify longer-term trends. Companies can proactively discover what product or features to build next, and which customer segments will most likely be receptive to them.

This customer-focused experience should carry through the entire customer lifecycle. Increasingly,

B2B buyers prefer an easier path not just to learn about and buy a product, but to find an easier way to get customer service. A study by Nuance Enterprise found that 75 percent of survey respondents said self-service is a convenient way to address customer service issues. Moreover, 67 percent said they preferred self-service to speaking with a company representative[9]. Self-service saves time, enhances the customer experience, improves retention, and builds loyalty.

Focusing on customer desires for self-service options to learn about, evaluate, purchase, and support their software product puts organizations in a position to satisfy customers and increase revenues and the user base. Personalizing the customer acquisition process can help customers realize the value of your product sooner, and stay with your company longer.

But what do we mean by personalized customer experience? In a nutshell, it's about relevance and context. Are you reaching the right customer and customer segment? Is your message contextual, and sent through the channel that is most convenient for the customer? Does your SaaS product track where a user left off? Is your pricing model and customer acquisition strategy personalized for different types of customers? Answering these questions will help your company deliver a truly individualized customer experience.

2.4 Why is Personalization Intrinsic to Customer Experience?

Personalizing the customer experience is another trend that spills over to SaaS from consumer industries. We see consumer companies tailoring our experiences, and we expect enterprise software companies to follow suit. Amazon records what items we viewed, and makes recommendations based on our buying behaviors. Netflix does the same by suggesting TV shows and movies that match our tastes. We see personalization becoming the essential part of a great customer experience. SaaS companies that adopt personalization as part of their strategy will reap disproportional benefits.

Personalization is a process of tailoring a service or product, message, experience, price, or preferred channel to accommodate a specific customer.

The personalization concept can be applied to a customer acquisition or retention process as well as to customer journeys. Let's see how it can improve conversion rates and shorten the sales cycle.

Customer experience is personalized when it is contextual. In other words, your organization needs to know enough about an individual buyer:

- Demographics
- Title
- Needs
- Account or organization that is evaluating your product
- Company size
- Company location
- Industry
- Preferred communications channel
- Activity to date on your website
- Engagement to date with your product

When we talk about behavior, we need to highlight two dimensions:

- Historical data that explains behavioral patterns of a customer
- Real-time behavioral data that can help your company experiment with and optimize interaction as it happens

We will further discuss how to create a personalized customer experience, but for now, it should be clear that effective personalization assumes a lot of knowledge about a prospect.

We will further discuss how to create a personalized customer experience, but for now, it should be clear that effective personalization assumes a lot of knowledge about a prospect.

Today, the majority of conversations about personalization in the SaaS industry revolve around personalizing marketing interactions – website content, e-mails, and marketing ads, among others. Organizations tend to think about personalization in relation to marketing only. It's just as important that the product, and everything else related to the customer experience, is personalized.

Let's get back to our example of Netflix and Amazon. We know intuitively as consumers that effective personalization comes from understanding how we interact with the actual product. The compounding effect of behavioral knowledge is what makes Netflix and Amazon so successful. The more companies learn about customers over the lifetime of a relationship, the more successfully they can create meaningful experiences. With actual data from customer interactions with the product, companies can segment customers into meaningful groups to personalize how they experience their product. The goal is to interact with each customer in a way that seems specifically tailored to them, but at scale.

SaaS products are no different from consumer products in this way; customer interactions and behaviors with a product are fundamental to delivering a better customer experience. If customer interactions provide such valuable data, why not let prospects interact with your product early in the buying process, and use this data to nurture them accordingly?

This is exactly what many organizations figured out, and why we see a growing number of SaaS companies providing self-service freemium products and free trials. Opening the door to the proverbial store allows companies to watch how customers explore it, what products attract more traffic, and how to interact with them to find out what they want.

Going forward, delivering such a personalized experience will be crucial for every SaaS company. Such an approach enables companies to build a competitive advantage and optimize how they drive revenue, CAC efficiency, renewals, and intelligent product development decisions. SaaS companies taking a more personalized approach to creating customer experience will lead the pack in the customer experience era.

Personalizing the customer experience becomes as important to SaaS company survival as it is for a consumer company. Let's look now at how SaaS companies can transform into customer-centric organizations.

Part II

How to Become a Customer-Experience-Focused Organization

"Unless commitment is made, there are only promises and hopes…but no plans."

PETER DRUCKER

Chapter 3
Show, Don't Tell

SaaS companies must commit to boosting their customer experience to survive. A personalized customer experience is difficult to achieve for multiple reasons. Companies must change how they think about customer experience, then redesign their organizations, policies, GTM strategies, and customer acquisition processes. Furthermore, this transition requires a strong understanding of the customer lifecycle, buying process, customer journeys, customer demographics, and behavioral data.

In this chapter, we cover six essential steps for evolving to become an experience-centric organization:

Old Way	New Way
Focus on the sales process	Focus on the buying process
Tell me about your product	Show, and let me try, your product
Align around funnels/product lifecycles	Align around customer lifecycles
Organize around individual interactions	Organize around complete journeys
Operate in siloed teams	Operate as a customer-experience-oriented organization
Execute on a traditional GTM strategy	Execute on a product-led GTM strategy

First, let's see how the customer acquisition process is changing.

3.1 The Buying Process Outweighs the Sales Process

Before the SaaS revolution, enterprise software companies were predominantly sales-driven, with the company speaking at length with a sales rep to get product information. The high-touch sales model was warranted, since customers were required to sign long-term, expensive contracts.

The subscription economy—with lower prices, ownership, and switching costs—has changed the customer acquisition model. Companies made educational and product-related content more accessible to prospective customers as they searched for more efficient ways to generate product awareness and demand. Prospects could then find, learn, and compare software products earlier in the buying process, way before they interacted with sales. In this way, content marketing and lead generation were established as primary strategies for companies to generate awareness and demand.

The rise of content marketing and lead nurturing brought us marketing automation solutions that promised, among other things, to calculate content marketing ROI. (Lead nurturing is a process of continual communication with a prospect until he or she is ready to buy.) The new marketing-led approach to customer acquisition promises to close the gap between marketing and sales. Marketing teams generate and nurture leads, while sales teams focus on prospects that are aware of a product and the problem it solves. A marketing-led approach has made SaaS companies far more efficient and effective. Eloqua, Marketo, and Hubspot are the most well-known examples of marketing automation companies that popularized a marketing-led strategy. When it comes to content marketing, Hubspot and Marketo set the standard. The amount of content created by these companies is startling.

Today, prospective customers progress far along the buying process before talking to sales, making content strategy a given. Content marketing helps prospects recognize the problem and need for the product while empowering them to evaluate alternatives and create a shortlist of potential solutions. Through content, buyers in the enterprise software market become more knowledgeable about industry products and trends. By the time your sales team interacts with a prospect, you can expect the prospect to have formed a perception of what your product does and available alternatives.

3.2 Why Traditional Customer Acquisition Falls Short

As business buyers, we often reach out to our professional and social networks for advice, or to simply ask for product recommendations. We read thought leadership content to learn about new ideas, expertise, and trends that are relevant for our decision-making. When we land on the website, we often are forced to share our contact information through lead forms in exchange for content, and then receive marketing e-mails notifying us about a new whitepaper, report, or webinar. As we come back and engage on a company's website or through e-mail, we receive calls from a sales development team whose job is to assess our level of pain and fit—and only then are we given access to a free trial, or guided through a proof-of-concept process. This is what we refer to as the traditional acquisition process.

Figure 3.1 shows a simplified version of the traditional customer acquisition process for SaaS companies as described. This is not a universal process, since not every company gates its free trial, and not every company provides one. Furthermore, there is a whole journey that companies have to design after a prospect becomes a customer. Nonetheless, one thing should be clear: a large part of the customer acquisition journey in the traditional customer acquisition process happens outside of the product.

Figure 3.1 - Traditional Customer Acquisition Process (Simplified)

Why isn't this approach very effective? Prospects are forced to fill out lead forms in exchange for content, or submit requests for a demo, and talk to a sales rep before accessing a free trial. In the consumer industry, the buying process rarely involves interaction with a company representative, and often just includes a self-service option. Enterprise buyers want the same frictionless experience in their professional lives. As a result, they are no longer willing to wait and jump through lead forms to try your software; they can—and will—turn around and try a competitor's trial instead.

And how can you blame them? Who wants to receive e-mails about your next webinar, or from your sales development rep asking for a quick chat to learn whether the solution is a good fit for you?

Another key reason why the traditional customer acquisition process isn't effective: It focuses more on the behavior of prospective customers outside of the product, rather than on in-product behavior. Think about the correlation between downloading a whitepaper, opening an e-mail or visiting a website, and the buyer's intention to purchase a product. Lead scoring in enterprise marketing was created to show that the leads they pass to sales are of a high quality. But can you truly say with much certainty that these buyer activities strongly indicate an intent to purchase?

Let's look at this process through the example of a consumer walking into a shoe store. Imagine that you have to talk to a sales clerk in front of the store and share your e-mail and other contact information just to walk in. Would you consider this a good customer experience? Additionally, who do you think shows a higher buying intent: someone who just walks around the store, or someone who stops to feel an Asics shoe or who asks to try a pair on?

3.3 Getting Personal is Paramount

SaaS companies that want to deliver great customer experience should pay close attention to these scenarios. In the SaaS world, a stellar customer experience depends on how well companies understand their behaviors in the product. Organizations that make it hard to evaluate and try their product irritate prospective customers with a subpar experience. Perhaps even worse, they limit their growth potential because they lose the opportunity to learn early on how customers interact with their product.

There is no better data for organizations to build a personalized customer experience than data that uncovers how prospects interact with their product.

Allowing prospects to sign up and try a product improves customer experiences, and provides teams with relevant behavioral data that helps them further personalize the experience—and that ultimately yields a loyal customer and higher lifetime value.

3.4 Buyers Want to Go It Alone

Research supports the idea that buyers want an easier way to evaluate and buy software products. According to Forrester Research, 59 percent of B2B buyers prefer not to interact with a sales rep[1], and 74 percent find buying from a website more convenient[2]. It may be too early to talk about the "death of a (B2B) salesman", but this data suggests a growing trend toward consumerization in business markets. The same way content marketing empowered prospective customers to self-educate, self-service allows them to evaluate a product. That's why more SaaS companies are moving toward free trials or a freemium model as starting points for engaging prospects.

Customer expectations could be summarized with an old saying: "Show, don't tell." In other words, "Don't tell me how great your product is; let me try your product and judge for myself."

3.5 Customer Experience Requires a New Way of Thinking and Acting

SaaS companies that want to succeed are embracing a new customer acquisition process. This involves providing the immediate option to sign up for a product freemium or free trial. Marketing, sales, customer success, and even product teams can then learn more about their prospective and existing customers through in-product interaction, allowing them to better personalize the experience.

Figure 3.2 shows how companies are changing the customer acquisition process by providing early access to their products. Again, let's point out that this is in no way a complete view; we will explain this process in more detail further in the book. Notice though, this new process flips the order of how companies interact with prospective customers. Successful teams put in place strategies that reduce the time from when a prospective customer lands on the website to the time the prospect signs up to use the product. These teams invite prospects into a proverbial store, limiting the barrier to entry by making the front door larger, always open, and welcoming.

Figure 3.2 - New Customer Acquisition Process (Simplified)

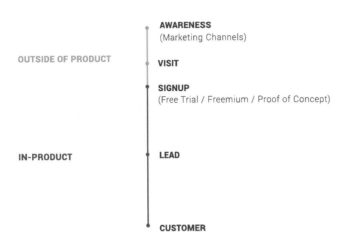

Using the store analogy, a sales rep in the shoe store can notice who exhibits more interest in what style of shoes, and then can offer help when he sees a customer pick up a shoe in the basketball section. It's not going to take long for consumer companies to personalize messages and ads. These could highlight relevant offers in the store and even lead someone to a specific department in the store based on that person's previous purchases. A text message might inform the customer that the shoe he tried but did not purchase last time is now on sale.

While online-first businesses—and enterprise SaaS companies in particular—use a different business model, they can call upon many technologies that enable them to personalize the buying process. Let's look at some very successful companies in the subscription era that led their customer acquisition by providing a free trial or freemium.

3.6 Embracing a Bottom-Up Sales Strategy

A great example is Trello, which offers a web-based project management solution. The team behind Trello grew its user base and revenue by providing a freemium option. The company targeted individuals in a professional setting, providing an easy way for them to try and purchase the product. In just six years, Trello passed 19 million users, and was later acquired by Atlassian for $425 million3. It's difficult to judge how much behavioral data was used by Trello teams to personalize customer experiences; and, of course, being a lightweight product with mass appeal made it easier to spark viral growth through a freemium offering. However, even tracking user adoption over a large set of users could be extremely valuable to a product team wanting to prioritize what needs to be built to accelerate growth.

Asana, the task management SaaS company, is another example of a company that brings customers inside the product sooner. Similarly, Zoom.us, the video conferencing solution, promotes only one call to action on its website: "Sign Up Free." Do you know what you won't find on the Trello, Asana, and Zoom websites? Lead forms. "Sign up" is the only door to enter the store, so to speak.

Trello, Zoom.us, and Asana drive customer acquisition with a bottom-up sales strategy, thus getting individuals in organizations to use their products first; and if the product is valuable for them, the rest of the organization is more likely to adopt it. Managers will be more inclined to subscribe to the product across the entire company when a large portion of employees are already using it. The success of this strategy requires companies to design customer experiences that make product adoption quick and inexpensive. This is what we mean by consumerization in SaaS: companies focus on showing value to individuals first, instead of selling products to managers or decision-makers who won't be using it on daily basis. It's worth noting that the freemium model isn't optimal for every company. Later in the book, we will discuss freemium and free trial models in more detail.

SaaS companies that understand customer expectations and experience are shifting to a new customer acquisition process. The goal is to reduce the time it takes, as well as the friction involved, for a buyer to try the product. This shift refocuses organizations to nurturing and personalization strategies that rely more on customer behaviors in-product. Figure 3.3 presents the comparison between the old and new customer acquisition models.

Figure 3.3 - Traditional vs. New Customer Acquisition Process (Simplified)

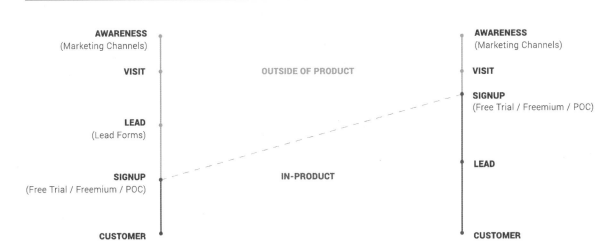

Another important difference: Companies that use the new customer acquisition approach can more confidently define a promising lead, because they base the determination on in-product behavior, rather than on the prospect's engagement with marketing content.

We already mentioned that this new acquisition process empowers teams to better personalize customer experiences and journeys. Prospects share important data with the company during the free trial, which the company can use to guide these prospects to realize initial product value. Companies can even use this data to entice those to come back and pick up where they left off using the product.

In the traditional customer acquisition process, companies rely on segmentation as the guide for personalizing the buyer experience. This is based mostly on demographic data about the prospects, firmographic data about their companies, and marketing behavioral data, such as what content was downloaded. The new customer acquisition strategy empowers teams to add significant in-product behavioral data to the formula, so they can guide prospects through even more personalized journeys—and ones that actually occur in the product.

Finally, let's not overlook the fact that in-product behavior can be insightful for marketing teams to improve the ROI of marketing campaigns. Sales teams can prioritize and focus on leads that are already using the product. The customer success team can understand where prospects are facing difficulties in using the product, and product teams can make more data-driven decisions on what features to build and what updates to release next.

In fairness, some enterprise software companies find it expensive and ineffective to offer a free trial or freemium; we cover these cases in Chapter 4. However, even SaaS companies that sell more technical and impactful solutions with higher price tags acknowledge the need for an easy, painless way for teams to try their products.

Zendesk and Splunk, for example, offer free trials. While a free trial removes some friction, Splunk still asks lots of questions during the free trial signup journey. We believe the trend of reducing barriers for business customers to try a product will accelerate as SaaS moves toward consumerization. We can hear the revolution on the street with slogans like "Show, don't tell. Let me try!"

Old Way	New Way
Companies forced prospects to jump through hoops, such as filling out lead forms or requesting a free trial, a quote, or a demo to learn about the product.	Companies provide access to products and personalization earlier in the buying cycle via free trials and signups for a freemium product.

Chapter 4
Taking an Outside-In Perspective of the Customer Lifecycle

In the beginning of the software revolution, and the early days of SaaS, the software development models resembled processes of the past century. These processes were based on concrete and easily understood requirements and assembly lines, as in the automobile industry. Agile methodologies in the early 2000s changed how companies design and deliver software products in two important ways.

First, agile methodologies emphasized shorter development cycles to minimize risk and ensure a shorter feedback loop from customers. Efficient cycles enabled companies to build software products more cost-effectively, while also letting customers experience and provide feedback about the product. This is in stark contrast to designing software that took months, or even years, to reach customers.

Second, agile shifted the focus from the product lifecycle to the customer lifecycle as the primary GTM strategy. This is a better way to understand customers' needs and communicate value through marketing and sales activities.

In much the same way, SaaS companies that are serious about customer experience will have to rethink how they look at the company-customer relationship. It's easier for companies to design sales processes, rather than put themselves in their customers' shoes. It may sound banal, but analyzing the buying process can profoundly affect an organization.

Back to the shoe store example: A store manager might create a policy to greet every customer who walks in, and tell them about a new golf shoe collection. But how effective would this policy be with a returning customer who bought four or five Asics Tigers in the last few years? While a simple consumer example, this helps illustrate how the way that customers buy can be quite different, and disconnected from how companies sell.

The SaaS revolution and the introduction of agile methodologies removed the need for companies to use product lifecycle as the way to market their product; but sales-driven thinking about customer journeys manifested in the new strategy of creating marketing and sales funnels. You probably can find a thousand different variations of a SaaS sales funnel, but most focus on the company's sales process, not the customer's buying journey.

In the past decade at least, there has been much talk about companies becoming customer-first and customer-centric; yet many enterprise software companies that call themselves customer-centric are failing at the first step of providing better customer experience. They fail to understand how customers buy, because they still focus on how they ought to be sold.

4.1 What is a Product Lifecycle?

> **Product lifecycle** is a framework that helps a company organize its marketing and sales of a product, from introducing it to the market to when sales peak and decline.

Figure 4.1 - Product Lifecycle Framework

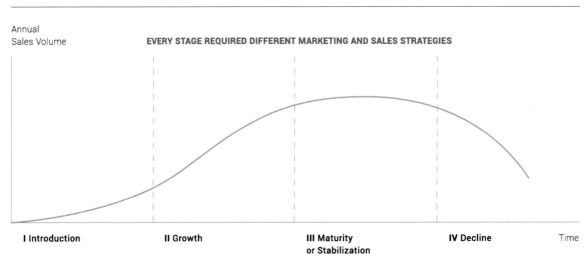

Figure 4.1 shows a classic product lifecycle diagram where each stage corresponds to specific sales and marketing strategies, programs, and campaigns[1].

It was helpful to see selling and marketing through the prism of the product lifecycle in the on-premise software era. At that time, it was more complicated and costly for companies to release updates, because often, new releases were treated as a new version of the product requiring a new physical installation of software. Just picture an early version of Windows that had to be updated using a CD, or even a floppy drive.

With SaaS, the product lifecycle concept became obsolete. Today, companies make incremental improvements and release product updates in the cloud on a weekly, daily, and sometimes even hourly basis. For example, Amazon releases new software every 11.6 seconds[2]! This became possible thanks to a new set of technologies called "continuous deployment".

Quick deployments of new software updates and features increase the speed at which companies receive customer feedback. A customer lifecycle framework puts customers at the center of virtually everything a company focuses on, to successfully operate and sustain revenue growth. The customer experience becomes an essential part of driving an effective customer engagement and GTM strategy that helps move prospective customers from one lifecycle stage to the next.

What Is the Customer Lifecycle?

Customer lifecycle is a framework that describes the process a customer goes through when considering, buying, using, and advocating use of a product or service.

Companies that understand how their customers progress through the lifecycle can not only better evaluate customer experiences at different points, they can also uncover critical steps where customers get stuck. For instance, perhaps prospective customers tend to abandon a trial upon hitting a certain step in a task they are trying to complete. By noticing this pattern, the company could investigate to determine the problem with the step, and then take measures to remedy the situation.

Furthermore, unlike a product lifecycle or marketing/sales funnel, a customer lifecycle is a continuous process of retaining, expanding, and creating loyal customers (as shown in Figure 4.2). Unfortunately, the shoe store analogy only takes us so far. But it would be nice if you could buy a pair of shoes and then upgrade their color while you were wearing them (perhaps, one day, a startup will solve even this). For all companies, it is much more profitable to keep a customer than to acquire a new one. The beauty for SaaS companies is that the SaaS business model, combined with a new approach to customer acquisition, makes it easier to retain customers.

Figure 4.2 - Customer Lifecycle Framework

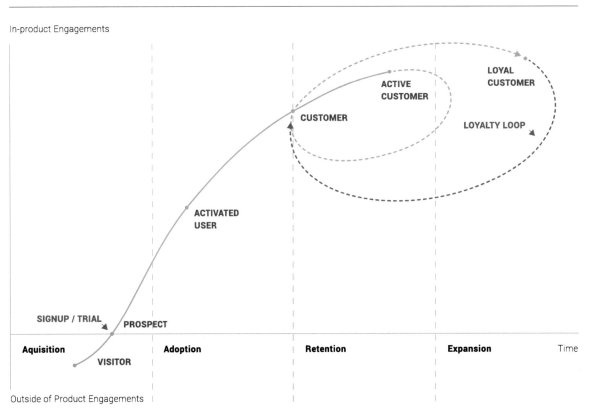

The customer lifecycle in Figure 4.2 is notably different from many other variations you can find. We included a y-axis to show whether a prospective customer has access to, and interacts with, the product at a particular stage. In other words, it shows in-product engagement. Ideally, you will see in-product engagement increase as prospects progress to the higher lifecycle stage. Signing up for a freemium or free trial signals that a site visitor has become a prospect. From this point, in-product engagement is a primary force behind the buyer moving along the lifecycle path.

The x-axis shows the time it takes for a prospect to progress. For example, the shorter the path from signup to becoming a customer, the more effective the organization is in acquiring customers—hence, the shorter the buying cycle.

In contrast, the simplified version of the customer acquisition process presented in Figures 3.1, 3.2, and 3.3 (customer lifecycle) underscores the importance of keeping customers and ensuring that they still derive value from your product over time. A paying customer does not always mean an active customer. Decline in product usage and engagement can be an early sign of a customer who will eventually churn.

In addition to taking into consideration metrics like customer satisfaction and Net Promoter Score (NPS), this customer lifecycle views customers as loyal after they renew their subscription for the first time.

4.2 The Four Stages of the SaaS Customer Lifecycle

Now, let's break down the four critical stages of a SaaS customer lifecycle: acquisition, adoption, retention, and expansion (modified based the following Customer Lifecycle framework)[3]:

Acquisition stage
The business goal is to influence prospects to try a product or service.

> CUSTOMER GOAL: Quickly assess pain-product fit and obvious benefits
> QUESTION: Does this product address my immediate needs?
> CUSTOMER ACTION: Signup/Trial
>
> CUSTOMER EXPERIENCE FOCUS:
- What customer segments should we engage, and what's the value of features we should be promoting?
- How can we reduce friction for buyers and influence them to try our solution?

Adoption stage
The business goal is to onboard prospects and showcase relevant value of the product.

> CUSTOMER GOAL: Learn how to use the product, evaluate it, and make a buying decision
> QUESTION: Is this product easy to use? Does it address my needs? Do I want to buy it?
> CUSTOMER ACTION: Onboarding/Initial value delivered/Convert to customer
>
> CUSTOMER EXPERIENCE FOCUS:
- How can we make customer experience a core value that our solution delivers?
- How can we accelerate and increase the trial-to-customer conversion rate?
- How can we nurture and re-engage customers with the product based on unique customer behaviors?

Retention stage

The business goal is to ensure that customers receive expected value from the product regularly, and possess knowledge about newly released product features and capabilities.

CUSTOMER GOAL: Receive value and benefit from the product

QUESTION: Do I still value and want to actively use this product? Is this product essential to achieving my personal and/or professional goals?

CUSTOMER ACTION: Daily Active User (DAU)/Monthly Active User (MAU)

CUSTOMER EXPERIENCE FOCUS:

- How can we ensure customers continuously receive value from using the product?
- How does customer behavior in the product help to prevent churn and predict CLV?

Expansion stage

The business goal is to influence customers to renew, increase product usage, purchase an upsell or cross-sell, and advocate use of the product.

CUSTOMER GOAL: Explore how to be more empowered and successful

QUESTION: Will I become more effective with increased product usage or new features?

CUSTOMER ACTION: Renewal/Upsell/Cross-sell/Advocate

CUSTOMER EXPERIENCE FOCUS:

- How can we deliver features and experiences that are more valuable to customers, and influence them to buy more or upgrade their subscription?
- How can we enable our customers to become public advocates?

Table 4.1 - Customer vs. Business Goals in Customer Lifecycle

	Customer Goal	Business Goal	Action/Metrics
Acquisition	Quickly assess pain-product fit and obvious benefits	Influence prospects to try a product or service	• Signup • Trial
Adoption	Learn how to use the product, evaluate, and make a buying decision	Onboard prospects and showcase relevant value of the product	• Onboarding • Initial value delivered • Convert to customer
Retention	Receive value and benefit from the product	Ensure that customers receive expected value from the product regularly and possess knowledge about newly released product features and capabilities	• Daily Active User (DAU)/ Monthly Active User (MAU)
Expansion	Explore how to be more empowered and successful	Influence customers to renew, increase product usage, upsell, cross-sell and advocate the product	• Renewal • Upsell • Cross-sell • Advocate

Table 4.1 summarizes customer and business goals for each stage of the lifecycle. When companies use a customer lifecycle framework, they can reevaluate their own processes to ensure that organizational goals are aligned with customer needs and expectations. From the customer lifecycle, we can infer the following:

- Every stage in the customer lifecycle corresponds to a specific need that must be addressed before a customer moves to the next stage, resulting in deeper engagement with a product and the company.
- Three out of four stages (adoption, retention, and expansion) occur while the customer uses the product. As a result, in-product behaviors and engagement and behavioral data should influence most of the customer journey throughout the lifecycle.
- The new customer acquisition process is closing the gap between the time the prospect and company engage in conversation, and the time the prospect tries the product.
- Retention and expansion stages in a customer lifecycle are a continuous process of

delivering value to the customer. See the highlighted "loyalty loop" in the customer lifecycle diagram (Figure 4.2).

- The earlier product lifecycle approach encouraged companies to focus on marketing and sales strategies based on where the product was in the cycle. Customer lifecycle puts customers at the center, and helps companies focus on how to market and sell software products in response to customer needs and preferences.

Why is understanding the customer lifecycle important to transitioning to a more personalized customer experience? A customer lifecycle framework forces companies to understand the buying process from the customer perspective. It enables companies to use in-product behaviors to deliver relevant experiences to each user, which helps acquire, retain, and grow the customer base.

When SaaS companies understand in-product customer journeys and where a customer is in the lifecycle, teams can segment customers into meaningful groups to address individual needs and goals. This strategy of understanding the behaviors that drive customers to the next lifecycle stage is more effective in increasing product adoption and engagement.

Old Way	New Way
Companies focused on product lifecycle as the primary framework to market and sell the product.	Companies focus on customer lifecycle as the primary framework to acquire, adopt, retain, and grow their customer base.

Chapter 5
Understanding the Whole Customer Journey

The customer lifecycle encompasses a complete company-customer relationship, from start to finish. In a sense, the customer lifecycle is like your complete life history, and includes birthplace, family history, childhood events, high school years, college, early career, starting a family, birth of children, retirement, and even death. Your life story is filled with journeys and important moments. If you went to college, that journey includes certain interactions and milestones that led you to graduate. Your college journey was filled with decisions and paths you took toward a certain career. In other words, a lifecycle includes many journeys, but there is a clear relationship between the two frameworks.

The customer lifecycle represents all the interactions and journeys a customer has with a company. Journeys, on the other hand, show a sequence of all touchpoints, interactions, and engagements of a customer before that person reaches a journey milestone. While lifecycle is a progression, the journey is the actual path.

The end of each meaningful journey is reaching a milestone. For example, the high school journey ends with graduation day. In SaaS, a free trial signup journey includes all steps that users must take to get inside the product for the first time. As buyers progress through one customer lifecycle stage to another, their journeys can be very unique. One may take a couple of days and four interactions between signing up to becoming fully onboarded. Another's onboarding journey could span a four-week period and contain twenty interactions.

> **The customer journey** is a series of all touchpoints a customer has with a company, brand, or product to reach a certain milestone.

Journeys can include digital and real-world touchpoints; they can span over many devices and channels.

Each prospective customer goes through unique steps when she evaluates and purchases software. This is why it is extremely challenging for companies to gain a complete picture of important journeys that lead customers to important milestones, such as completing onboarding, using your product for the first time, purchasing the product, reaching daily active user status, or renewing.

But the challenge is also in recognizing an optimal pattern.

While individual customer journeys can vary greatly from one customer to another, SaaS companies need to understand the overall pattern. Pattern analysis helps companies understand the most common journey, as well as critical outliers or bottlenecks that prevent prospects from reaching the next stage in the lifecycle.

Improving the customer experience starts with the company understanding its customer lifecycle. The next step is evaluating current journeys, and designing new optimal ones that lead customers to desired outcomes and milestones. Only when an organization understands the complete lifecycle and primary journeys can it effectively design individual touchpoints and interactions. Research suggests companies that focus on customer journeys before designing individual touchpoints are much more successful at enhancing the overall customer experience1. That's because more touchpoints can make the journey more complex. Overseeing the journey helps teams evaluate the need for each standalone touchpoint, and eliminate any unnecessary ones.

Designing interactions and engagements without outlining the journey can often result in high customer satisfaction with individual touchpoints, but low satisfaction across the journey2.

One way companies can improve the customer experience is to break down the customer path along the lifecycle into meaningful journeys that act as guideposts. While companies can rarely fully control customer journeys, designing the optimal journey is a great first step. The optimal journey is the shortest and most convenient path for prospective customers to reach the goal.

To summarize, the process of transitioning to a customer-experience company follows these steps:

- **CUSTOMER LIFECYCLE.**
  What is the customer lifecycle for our most profitable customers? How can we make this lifecycle as rewarding and frictionless as possible?
- **CUSTOMER JOURNEYS.**
  What are the most important customer journeys? What milestones advance the customer along the lifecycle?
- **TOUCHPOINTS, INTERACTIONS, AND ENGAGEMENTS.**
  What are the most optimal touchpoints and interaction for each customer journey? Can some be eliminated or simplified?

It's impossible to overstate the importance of understanding customer journeys for enabling a new customer acquisition approach. Enticing prospects to evaluate and try a product via self-service free trials or freemiums opens a unique opportunity for SaaS companies. It enables them to track and optimize in-product journeys that move prospective customers to important milestones, such as realizing initial product value.

Therefore, monitoring customer journeys is a crucial step. Instead of looking at just a part of a transaction or experience, the customer journey documents the full experience of being a customer.

5.1 Tracking Customer Journeys

A customer journey can consist of online and offline interactions. Digital (or online) touchpoints can happen outside of a product, or in-product. Remember, in Figure 3.1, the x-axis divides the customer lifecycle into out-of-product and in-product engagement areas.

We've explored the shift of SaaS companies away from lead generation forms that focus on customer journeys and interactions outside of their product to free trials and signups that focus on in-product customer journeys.

Let's focus on IN-PRODUCT CUSTOMER JOURNEYS, as they are the most effective way for a prospective customer to experience true value from the product as they move along their customer lifecycle.

> **In-product customer journey** is a sequence of all touchpoints that a customer has inside the product.

Providing customers access to the product early in the acquisition stage reduces the reliance of teams on non-product customer engagements. It also increases the importance of product engagements. Table 5.1 shows examples of in-product and out-of-product engagements.

Table 5.1 - In-Product vs. Outside-of-product Customer Engagements

Customer Engagements	
In-product	**Out-of-product**
• LOGS IN	**Online:**
• SETS UP A FREE TRIAL	
• PROVIDES IN-PRODUCT FEEDBACK AND COMPLETES SURVEYS	• DOWNLOADS A WHITEPAPER OR INDUSTRY REPORT FROM THE COMPANY'S WEBSITE
• COMPLETES ONBOARDING	• REGISTERS FOR A WEBINAR
• USES A CERTAIN PRODUCT FEATURE	• VISITS PRICING PAGE, FAQS, OR DOCUMENTATION PAGES
• ADDS A TEAM MEMBER	• OPENS SALES OR NEWSLETTER E-MAILS
• INTEGRATES WITH THIRD-PARTY SERVICE	• INTERACTS WITH COMPANY ON SOCIAL MEDIA
	Offline:
	• TALKS TO CUSTOMER SUPPORT/CUSTOMER SUCCESS ON THE PHONE

Let's illustrate how we think about customer journeys at Aptrinsic. For this purpose, we'll compare the in-product journeys of Prospect A and Prospect B through the acquisition and adoption stages of the customer lifecycle. Both journeys include out-of-product and in-product touchpoints and interactions.

At Aptrinsic, we define initial value as when a prospect installs our JavaScript (JS) code and starts collecting product analytics data. The optimal customer journey to reach this milestone follows this sequence:

- VISIT WEBSITE
- SIGN UP FOR FREE TRIAL
- COMPLETE THE PRODUCT TUTORIAL
- SET UP PRODUCT
- INSTALL JS CODE INTO THE PRODUCT

Now, let's review two hypothetical journeys by two prospects: John and Danielle.

John starts the journey by clicking on a social media post, then visits the website and signs up for a free trial; the website visit is a non-product engagement. The free trial signup identifies John as a prospect, and from that point, we track all product interactions. John completes the onboarding tutorial, but leaves right after.

We send a reminder e-mail to him; John opens it, but doesn't return to the product. Two days later, we send another reminder to entice John to come back, create a product, and install JS code. This time, John returns to the app and creates a new product that generates a unique code. Since we are not collecting any data for John's product, we know he didn't install JS code, so we send a reminder e-mail. The next day, Aptrinsic starts collecting analytics data for John's product, which means he installed the JS code. The journey to realize initial value is complete. Reaching this milestone allows John to track and analyze his product inside of Aptrinsic. It also allows us to track his product usage and optimize his engagement.

Overview of John's journey:

1   CLICKED ON SOCIAL MEDIA POST

2   VISITED WEBSITE

3   COMPLETED SIGNUP/FREE TRIAL

4   COMPLETED ONBOARDING TUTORIAL

5   OPENED NURTURING E-MAIL (NOT RETURNED TO THE PRODUCT)

6   OPENED REMINDER E-MAIL (NO ACTIVITY FOR 2 DAYS)

7   SET UP PRODUCT

8   OPENED E-MAIL REMINDER TO INSTALL JS

9   INSTALLED JS CODE, DATA COLLECTED

Figure 5.1 represents a 9-step process that John took to reach the milestone of collecting product usage analytics. It should be clear that touchpoints 1, 2, 5, 6, and 8 happened outside of the product. Touchpoints 5, 6, and 8 are e-mail reminders triggered by John's inactivity.

Figure 5.1 - John's Journey to Initial Value

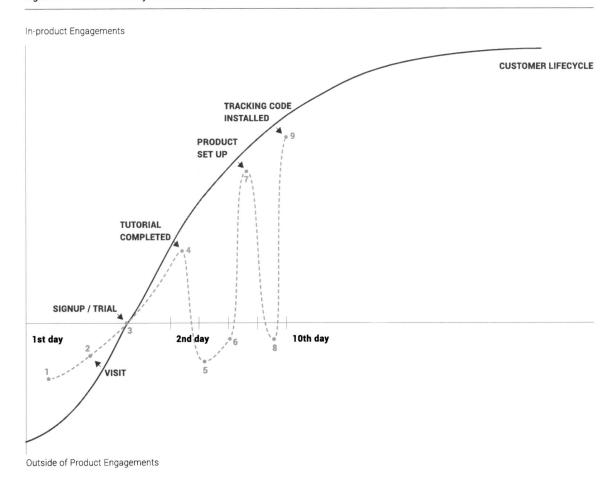

John completed this journey in 10 days:

1ST DAY: VISIT, SIGNUP, ONBOARDING TUTORIAL

2ND-3RD: DAY NO ACTIVITY

4TH DAY: E-MAIL REMINDER

5TH-6TH: DAY NO ACTIVITY

7TH DAY: E-MAIL REMINDER, CREATED NEW PRODUCT (GENERATED JS CODE)

8TH-9TH DAY: NO ACTIVITY

10TH DAY: E-MAIL REMINDER, TRACKING CODE IMPLEMENTED, DATA COLLECTED

In this hypothetical scenario, John received two reminder e-mails to create a new product, and one reminder e-mail to install JS code. All three e-mails were triggered by John's inactivity, and all three guided him to continue the journey where he left off. Now, let's compare this journey with the journey taken by Danielle.

Danielle starts with the same touchpoint as John, and signs up for a free trial; but unlike John, Danielle engages with the product right away using essential product features that showcase the initial product value to first-time users. During the initial free trial signup, Danielle completes onboarding and creates a new product that generates a unique JS code. She then logs in to the product the next day and receives an in-product notification to install the JS code and start collecting product analytics data.

Overview of Danielle's journey:

1   **VISITED WEBSITE**
2   **COMPLETED SIGNUP/FREE TRIAL**
3   **COMPLETED ONBOARDING TUTORIAL**
4   **SET UP PRODUCT**
5   **LOGGED INTO PRODUCT AND RECEIVED IN-PRODUCT REMINDER**
6   **INSTALLED JS CODE, DATA IS COLLECTED**

Figure 5.2 shows a step-by-step journey for Danielle to reach initial value as we define it at Aptrinsic.

Figure 5.2 - Danielle's Journey to Initial Value

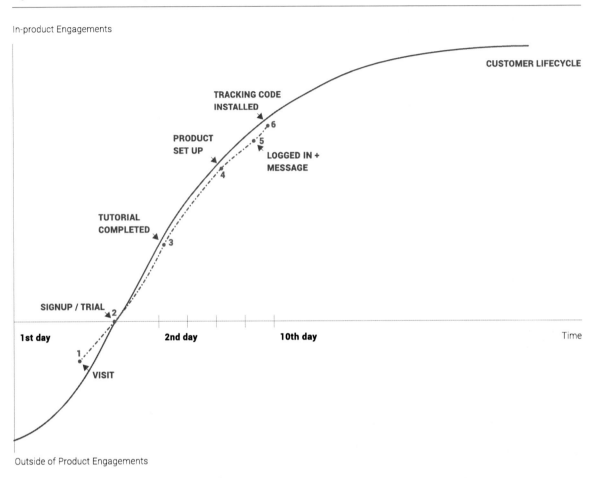

In this scenario, Danielle completed the journey in two days, with fewer touchpoints:

1ST DAY: VISIT, SIGNUP, TUTORIAL, CREATED NEW PRODUCT

2ND DAY: LOGGED IN, SAW IN-PRODUCT REMINDER, INSTALLED TRACKING CODE

Table 5.2 lists all the steps in the journeys of the two prospects. Danielle completed these steps in a much shorter timeframe, which could indicate a higher buying intent.

Table 5.2 - In-product Journeys for John and Danielle

John's Journey	Danielle's Journey
In-product	**Out-of-product**

	John's Journey		Danielle's Journey
1	CLICK	1	VISITED WEBSITE
2	CIAL MEDIA POST	2	COMPLETED SIGNUP/FREE TRIAL
3	VISITED WEBSITE	3	COMPLETED ONBOARDING TUTORIAL
4	COMPLETED SIGNUP/FREE TRIAL	4	SET UP PRODUCT
5	COMPLETED ONBOARDING TUTORIAL	5	LOGGED INTO THE PRODUCT
6	OPENED NURTURING E-MAIL		AND RECEIVED IN-PRODUCT REMINDER
	(NOT RETURNED TO THE PRODUCT)	6	INSTALLED JS CODE, DATA IS COLLECTED
7	OPENED REMINDER E-MAIL		
	(NO ACTIVITY FOR 2 DAYS)		
8	SET UP PRODUCT		
9	OPENED E-MAIL REMINDER		
	TO INSTALL JS		
10	INSTALLED JS CODE, DATA IS COLLECTED		

Figure 5.3 shows both journeys in the context of the customer lifecycle. We gave an example of just one journey type, but as prospects progress, the next journey will lead them to set up our product mapper. When that step is completed, the prospect will be guided to design and launch an onboard experience; and the journey to the fourth milestone will be complete when the prospect creates and sends the first e-mail or in-product message.

The velocity with which a prospect moves through the lifecycle to reach the next stage is a very important factor to consider and prioritize. Shorter time to value will likely correlate with higher probability to close and to become a highly satisfied DAU.

Figure 5.3 - Optimal Journey to Initial Value

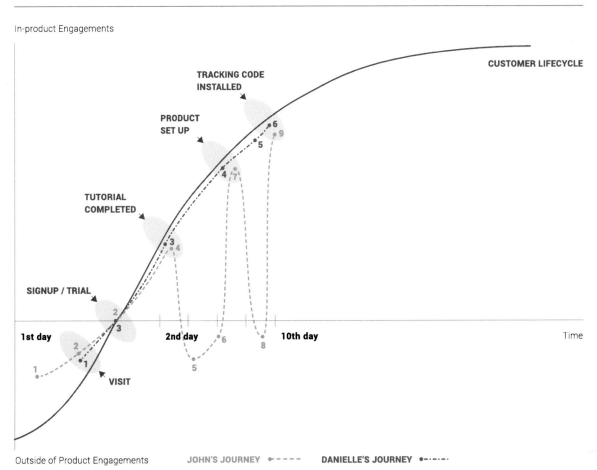

If we plotted many customer journeys into the customer lifecycle, we could identify the optimal path to initial value. Additionally, we could understand better the average time it takes to travel this journey, and steps where prospects get lost or fall off. Customer journey analysis provides companies with tremendous insight into understanding and optimizing journeys that directly impact the overall customer experience.

Every touchpoint and interaction along the journey is an opportunity for the company to influence the prospective customer's impression and create a deeper relationship between the company and prospective customer. This is what could be referred to as a Moment of Truth.

A Moment of Truth (MOT), in marketing, is the moment when a customer/user interacts with a brand, product, or service in a way that serves to form or change an impression about that brand, product, or service.

Potentially, every touchpoint in the journeys of John and Danielle is a moment of truth.

5.2 Mind the Value Gap!

Not every prospect who signs up for a free trial becomes a customer; and not every customer will renew the subscription. Let's look again at the journey of John. During the initial signup, he completed the product tutorial, but then left and didn't return to product for four days, until he received the second e-mail reminder.

But in many cases, users leave the product, never to return after the initial signup. Often prospective customers' needs are not met because the product doesn't provide enough value, or because the prospective customer expected something completely different.

> "Customers attach value to products in proportion to the perceived ability of those products to help solve their problems."
> – THEODORE LEVITT, THE MARKETING IMAGINATION

This is what we call a Value Gap. It is a difference between expected and delivered (or perceived) value. John might have never returned to the product after completing the onboarding tutorial. Maybe, in that case, he expected something different from the product, or the tutorial didn't do a good job enticing him to complete the next steps to realize the value from the product.

A **Value Gap** is the discrepancy between what a customer expects from the product and the value received or perceived.

The perception of value is as important as the value itself. If, for example, if a prospect doesn't know how to use your product or has an incorrect perception of its value, the result can be a Value

Gap that will influence the prospect's behavior and buying decision.

A Value Gap can happen for many reasons, but here are some big ones:

1. Product fails to provide adequate value
2. Customer is the wrong fit for the product
3. Customer doesn't understand a product's capabilities or how to use it
4. Customer experiences something jarring or painful (i.e., confusion, dissatisfaction, competitive incentive, etc.) that changes their perception while using the product

In the first scenario of the product not actually showing enough value, the company needs to go back to the drawing board and radically change the product to increase real and perceived value in the eyes of prospective customers. If a prospect is a wrong fit for the product, the problem may be that your marketing and outbound sales team is focusing on the wrong customer segments.

In the third and fourth scenarios, the company fails to communicate value through product capabilities/experience, and doesn't educate prospects on how to effectively use the product. To address these issues, teams can create a wide variety of product engagements and customer-centric journeys, to guide customers from first product touch to initial value.

In the example of John and Danielle's journeys, we defined initial value as a milestone when the prospect installs tracking code and starts collecting product analytics data. This data is the first step to understand how our product works, and to realize initial value. The concept of initial value is closely related to the Desired Outcome[3] concept, described in detail by customer success expert Lincoln Murphy.

Initial value is when a customer first experiences product value.

Realizing initial product value is the first step toward understanding how a product is intended to work, and what problem it was designed to solve. SaaS companies must carefully design the journey toward realizing initial value, as it is one of the most important journeys. This is the first time a user interacts with your product, and it's a real moment of truth. Companies not only need to identify the initial value, but also design optimal customer journeys that deliver it in a timely manner.

We will come back to discussing initial value when we talk about onboarding later in the book. But for now, let's see how different companies define initial value:

- For Asana, initial value can mean creating a new project, with tasks successfully assigned to a team member.
- For Zoom.us, it can mean signing up, organizing, and holding the first video conference.
- For Expensify, it could be creating the first expense report that is approved for payment.
- For Aptrinsic, initial value is delivered when a customer signs up, installs our tracking JS, and starts receiving product usage data from their customers.

The shorter the time to initial value, the more likely it is that a prospect will stay long enough to become a customer. In the scenarios we used, Danielle realized value in much less time than John.

5.3 What are Value or Golden Features?

Value Gap is often a result of the failure by prospects to complete journeys and interact with the most important product features.

Value features—sometimes known as "golden features"—are a set of product features that a prospect or customer must use to realize value and advance to the next stage of the customer lifecycle. During customer acquisition and adoption, value features guide prospects through a core use case, which is a common customer journey that users experience on a regular basis. Think back to the Aptrinsic example, and the way we guide prospects to install JS code to start collecting data. Prospects who experience value features are more likely to convert to customers.

When an activated user's product engagement declines, it causes a Value Gap. To close the gap, the company needs to immediately re-engage the customer.

Figure 5.4 - Value (Golden) Features and Value Gap

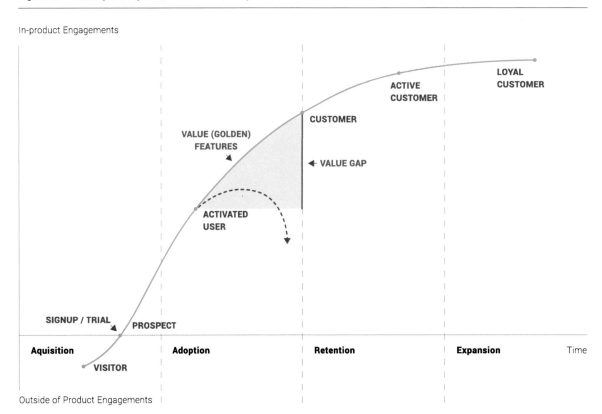

Figure 5.4 illustrates a Value Gap that an activated user can experience as a result of not engaging with product's most valued features. Let's point out a couple of important things regarding Value Gap and value features.

First, SaaS companies need to identify when a prospective customer's engagement changes—or potentially changes—in adverse ways, why it happened, and what features weren't used.

Companies can automate timely responses based on these behavioral insights in order to re-engage customers in meaningful ways, such as educating and reminding them about value features. We call this an ENGAGEMENT LOOP, which is a practice of using insightful in-product usage data, along with engagement tactics, to influence prospects and customers to re-engage with the product and experience more value.

In essence, customer lifecycle optimization means creating an ongoing process of sensing and responding to customer behaviors and feedback. The rate of growth in SaaS correlates with how effectively the company is creating loyal customers who renew or purchase higher subscription levels. We call this a LOYALTY LOOP, a continuous process of delivering substantial value and customer experience to keep customers using the product, adopting new features, increasing usage, and renewing.

Companies that master the process of creating loyal customers increase CLV and competitive advantage. Out of all tangible and intangible assets that your company has, customer loyalty is only one of three items that can't be easily copied by your competitors, according to **MARKETING: A LOVE STORY—HOW TO MATTER TO YOUR CUSTOMERS BY BERNADETTE JIWA**. Reputation and trust are the other two.

5.4 Key Takeaways

- An in-product customer journey is a set of all prospect/customer touchpoints inside the product.
- Giving prospective customers access to the product early in the acquisition stage reduces a marketing team's reliance on engagements outside the product and increases the importance and impact of product engagements.
- While they're in the product, prospects and customers are more likely to experience a MoT, when they form or change an impression about the brand, product, or service.
- A Value Gap occurs when there's a discrepancy between what the customer expects from the product and the value he or she actually receives or perceives.
- The company then must re-engage the customer right away to close the gap.
- An Engagement Loop uses product usage data to influence prospects and customers to re-engage.
- A Loyalty Loop delivers substantial value and experience to keep customers using the product and adopting new features, leading eventually to renewal.
- The initial value unit is an engagement, or set of engagements, that advances the customer through a core use case. Valued (golden) features are ones a prospect or customer must use to realize initial value.

Old Way	New Way
Companies failed to track customer journeys, instead focusing on individual interactions.	Companies manage and optimize customer journeys.
Companies failed to respond in a timely manner to customer engagement trends.	Companies can sense and respond in real time to customer activities and engagements.
Companies failed to track usage of product features.	Companies monitor and analyze product usage and product features, and how they impact customer experience and lifetime value.

Chapter 6
From Silos to a Cross-Functional Focus on Customer Experience

As we touched upon earlier in the book, the customer acquisition process in the on-premise and early SaaS eras was predominately sales-driven. Sales teams were primarily responsible for driving revenue. As information about products became more available, companies started bringing marketing closer to sales in order to close the gap between prospect exposure to content and messages, and nurturing them to be sales-ready. Marketing was responsible for driving the content strategy and campaigns to generate and nurture leads, and the sales organization was divided into three branches: sales development representatives (SDRs), responsible for qualifying prospects; account executives, responsible for closing deals; and customer success, responsible for keeping the customer long-term. The last of the three branches, customer success, became a department of its own.

In many organizations, that means enterprise buyers are interacting with three or four departments, depending on whether you consider SDRs to be a separate group. Each department sends its own e-mails and manages prospect interactions, making it difficult to keep track of the overall customer experience.

To deliver a stellar customer experience, companies have to rethink how departments collaborate. The first step in understanding the customer experience is to change from a sales process perspective to a buyer process perspective. Companies that understand the buying process from the customer's perspective are better positioned to develop great customer experiences.

Customer lifecycle thinking helps teams and departments understand and respond to how prospects and customers buy.

Let's be clear: Customer lifecycle is about understanding the buying process from the perspective of the customer, rather than a sales process from the perspective of the seller. It's a very important distinction, because when organizations focus on the buying processes, it forces them to carefully examine a customer's journey. Customer lifecycle bubbles up critical questions, like:

Why do customers and organizations buy what they buy?

How do they buy?

Unfortunately, many companies are still organized around a GTM and sales process that results in disconnected from customer experiences. Just as on-premise and early SaaS companies did, most of today's SaaS companies divide their complex GTM/sales process among specialized departments—marketing, sales, and customer success.

Traditionally, marketing is responsible for generating awareness and interest in the form of leads. Lead nurturing also falls under marketing. Sales teams close deals, and customer success oversees the customer onboarding process post-transaction, ensuring customer satisfaction, which ultimately is measured by retention and churn rates.

6.1 The Traditional Customer Handoff is Ineffective

Figure 6.1 shows that each team is responsible for only part of the customer lifecycle. A prospective customer is passed from one department to another. Marketing views the prospect as a lead and passes it to the Sales Development Representative (SDR) team. An SDR qualifies a prospect and hands it off to the account executive (AE) for demo and closing. The AE sends newly signed customers to the customer success team, which is responsible for keeping the customer happy. No wonder it can be tricky monitoring and managing overall customer experiences with the company and product!

Figure 6.1 - Customer Handoffs in the Customer Lifecycle

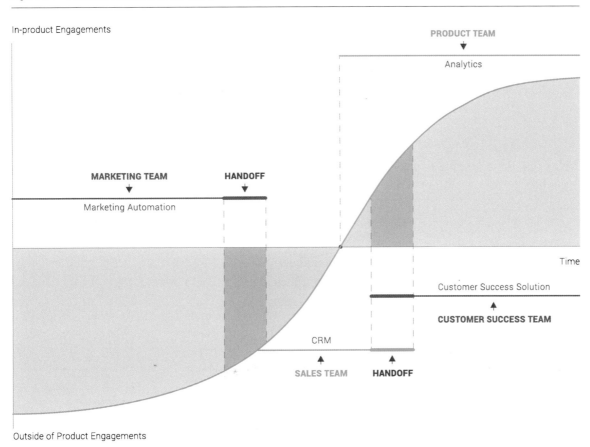

When a company experiences high customer churn rates, the first inclination is to look at what's wrong in the customer success department. Rarely does an organization look into marketing and sales to evaluate how these teams acquire customers and communicate with them, and how they impact customer expectations and behavior. Some questions to consider:

Does your marketing team target the right customers and communicate appropriate value?

Does your sales team qualify and close the right customers without overpromising?

Further, each department has goals and incentives that are aligned only with the part of the customer lifecycle for which they are responsible. The marketing team is incentivized based on leads; sales is based on demos and closed deals; customer success on churn rate and renewals. A sole focus on department goals can cause a disjointed customer experience when, for example, a customer receives multiple e-mails—from marketing telling them about an upcoming webinar, from the customer success team notifying them about their upcoming renewal, and from the product team informing them about a new feature release.

On top of that, each department is likely to use its own technology to send customer communications. This adds to the issue of a broken customer experience, since integration between the systems is often poor or non-existent.

The goals and incentives of each functional team should be considered based on how it impacts the overall customer experience and CLV. In his book Sales Acceleration Formula, Mark Roberge explains how Hubspot changed sales compensation plans to address a growing customer churn rate1. This is the first and critical step of sales and customer success teams: sharing responsibility for CLV and churn rate. But what about product and marketing teams? Should they be responsible for these metrics as well? We think so.

6.2 Why Aren't Product Teams More Involved in the Customer Acquisition Process?

Just as marketers in SaaS were brought closer to sales and made increasingly more responsible for revenue-related metrics, product managers will have to become part of the customer acquisition process. Unfortunately, in most organizations, product teams are not part of the process. When the product team is removed from the customer acquisition process, product analytics and customer behavioral data are missing from consideration to guide customers through lifecycle stages. Additionally, how does the organization know if the product is causing a customer acquisition problem? How long does it take for the marketing, sales, and customer success teams to determine and convince the broader organization that the product might be the cause of a failing customer acquisition strategy?

The disconnect between product teams and other key customer-facing teams (marketing, sales, and customer support) is similar to the long-standing disconnect between marketing and sales. At the end of the day, every department in a customer-focused organization should be involved in relevant customer-related activities. In the case of product teams, this means making them an integral part of customer acquisition tactical planning and execution.

Product experiences are an essential part of the customer experience. That's why product leaders need to understand the buying process, and what features are driving the value and adoption. In some organizations, product leaders are tasked with the goal of increasing average selling price (ASP). Specifically, they must decide which product features will be valued higher and could increase ASP.

Undoubtedly, the marketing, sales, customer success, and product teams should all be responsible for the customer experience. It is not easy to do. The key is for organizations to align goals and metrics around the customer experience across departments. Then they must find a way to aggregate customer data across multiple technologies. By taking these steps, they will be in a better position to design personalized customer engagements.

Figure 6.2 - Multiple Teams Contribute to the Customer Experience

6.3 Unified Customer Profile Data is Essential to Stellar Customer Experiences

The siloed organization is only one reason why creating a great customer experience is difficult for most organizations. This isn't a new problem, but it has a serious effect.

Historically, enterprise software vendors structured solutions to target a particular department and decision-maker, so each department relied on its own primary software solution to help manage workflows. This only reinforces the silos. Not only are departments driven by different goals and incentives, they often use different systems to manage and track customer interactions and relationships.

Marketing teams work with marketing automation tools; sales teams rely heavily on CRM systems; and customer success teams now call upon their own category of products to manage accounts and predict customer segments that are at risk of churning.

To be successful at providing a personalized customer experience, your organization needs a single system of record for all customer profile, company, and behavioral data. However, aggregating this data can be a very complicated process. Even if your company manages to piece all the relevant data together, it's rarely the case that product usage data can be attributed to an individual customer. New solutions (e.g. Zapier and Segment), which help companies connect APIs between different tools, can be useful. However, these API solutions are not robust enough to fully solve this problem, and instead create a "shadow IT"[3] effect as departments and individuals find their own workarounds to get their jobs done. And the challenges do not end here. In-product customer behavior data is difficult to access and align with customer production data and account data that lives in the CRM system.

Wondering if your organization is suffering because of these issues? Ask yourself these questions:

How often do your top 20 percent of customers, based on annual contract, log in to your product?

What are the top in-product journeys for these customers, from adoption to expansion?

What are the top three features that these customers use?

How quickly can you design messages to engage a customer or showcase your new features?

What features cause customers to stop using the product?

Where in the top three customer journeys are your prospects and clients getting stuck?

If you can't answer these questions, you don't have the holistic view you need of a customer's interactions across departments, or a whole picture of their product usage.

Historically, CRM systems are the default customer data warehouse. But CRMs weren't designed to enable teams to build multi-channel customer engagement based on the comprehensive customer profile data that includes in-product behavioral data.

A product analytics solution can help teams understand how users engage with the product, but these solutions are often missing the customer engagement piece—or worse, they can't really connect in-product behavioral data with account data (subscription details, customer lifecycle stage) and profile data (name, title).

Organizations need a unified, 360-degree collection of data, generated by pros-pects and customers while using the product, that can serve as a single source of truth.

Unified customer data should include these details:

- Profile data: name, title, contact information
- Company data (a.k.a. firmographics): size, subscription level, support tickets for all organizations and regions
- Behavioral data: daily/monthly active users, number of logins over a period of time, number of completed core use cases, number of features interacted with

To align departments around the customer lifecycle and customer experiences, companies need to bring product teams closer to the customer and the customer acquisition process. This unified data is a critical step.

6.4 From Department Goals to Customer-Centric Goals

In addition, organizations must align marketing, sales, customer success, and product teams on how to design and deliver effective customer experiences.

The first step is to tie customer experience metrics to the core objectives and goals of each department. CLV is one of the best metrics to measure and evaluate the long-term health of customer relationships. Net Promoter Score (NPS) is another metric that measures customer satisfaction and how customers value the experience with your product and company.

For example, marketing teams not only need to drive awareness via product trials and signups, but also track if prospects are becoming high-value customers. Revenue is a primary goal for sales teams, but CLV should also be used to evaluate the team's performance.

That's why metrics that measure the health of customer relationships, such as CLV, should also be connected to incentives. As a guide, look at how Hubspot changed its sales compensation plan to reflect CLV4.

Bottom line: We believe the product department should be involved in the customer acquisition process, and we believe every department involved in that should connect their goals, objectives, and incentives to CLV as a primary metric to evaluate long-term customer experience and satisfaction. We will discuss this topic in more detail in a later chapter.

Table 6.1 summarizes the metrics each department traditionally tracks through-out the customer acquisition process.

Table 6.1 - Departments Traditionally Involved in Customer Acquisition

	Marketing	Sales		Customer Success (CS)
		Sales Development Representatives (SDR)	**Account Executives (AE)**	
Goals	• Generate and nurture Marketing-Qualified Leads (MQLs)	• Convert MQLs into SQL/Demos	• Convert Demos into closed deals	• Onboard, train, renew, upsell, and cross-sell customer
Activities	• Generate content, campaigns, and ads • Organize events and webinars	• Conduct prospect qualification calls • Develop outbound sales campaigns	• Conduct demos • Develop relationships	• Design customer onboarding process • Develop workflow to re-engage with existing customers
Metrics	• MQLs • Signups/Trials • CAC	• Number of demos • MQL-to-SQL/ Demo conversion rate	• Closed deals • Demo-to-customer conversion rate • Average revenue per customer (ARPC)	• Churn rate • Renewal rate • NPS
Technology	• Marketing Automation	• CRM	• CRM	• CS Solutions

As you probably noticed, the product team is missing from this equation. In Table 3.5, below, we've added the product team to show how its goals, activities, and metrics fit with the whole customer acquisition process. You'll see a metric referred to as PQL. That's a Product-Qualified Lead. We'll explore this in more detail later in this chapter. For now, know that it's defined as a prospect that signed up and demonstrated buying intent based on product interest, usage, and behavioral data. Note also that SDRs shift from simply converting MQLs to helping and guiding users. This is an important distinction, and critical to success in the product-led, customer experience era.

Table 6.2 - Customer Experience Driven Departments Involved in Customer Acquisition

	Product Team	Marketing	Sales		Customer Success (CS)
			Sales Development Representatives (SDR)	Account Executives (AE)	
Goals	Create and update product and GTM messaging that attracts customers and solves their problems	Generate product signups and nurture users until they are ready to buy (becoming PQL)	Helping and guiding users; convert MQLs into SQLdemos	Convert PQLs into closed deals	Onboard, train, renew, upsell, and cross-sell customer
Activities	Manage product development strategy and vision Design GTM strategy and communication	Generate content, campaigns, and ads Organize events and webinars	Conduct prospect qualification calls Develop outbound sales campaigns	Conduct demos Develop relationship	Design customer onboarding process Develop workflow to re-engage with existing customers
Metrics	DAU MAU CLV	Signups/trials CAC CLV/signup/trial CAC vs. CLV	Number of PQLs MQL-to-SQL/demo con-version rate CLV/Demo	Close deals Demo-to-customer conversion rate ARP CLV vs. ARPC	Churn rate Renewal rate NPS CLV

How does this all relate to a personalized customer experience? It's about creating alignment and insight to meet and exceed customer expectations.

Table 6.3 - Organizations Must Be Equipped to Deliver a Personalized Customer Experience

Incentives	Everyone has a stake in customer acquisition, retention and growth —supported by training and incentives.			
CX Goals	CLV			
Technology	Product Analytics	Marketing Automation	CRM	Customer Success Solutions
Customer Profile Data	Customer Profile Data Warehouse and Engagement Solution (including in-product behavioral and production data)			
Questions to Develop Personalized CX	Do you know what to build and how to assess success/ failure of your features?	Do you know what features are more valuable and need to be promoted?	Do you know what features (and to whom) your team should be selling?	Do you know which customer is about to churn, or is losing value from your product?

When department goals and objectives are aligned around customer experience metrics, needs and vision, and unified customer profile data combining in-product behavioral, profile, and company data, cross-functional teams can create and deliver personalized customer experiences. Let's look at how team goals are changing, and how C-level executives are adjusting:

Old Way	New Way
Chief Product Officer (CPO): Know how customers use your product and what product features to build next. Design effective GTM strategy.	**CPO:** Analyze customer journeys and comprehensive customer data (including profile, firmographics, and behavioral) to make informed decisions on what to build next. Design and execute GTM strategy based on real-time product usage data.

Old Way	New Way
Chief Marketing Officer (CMO): Generate demand (Marketing-Qualified Leads [MQLs])—and nurture prospects through content and paid channels.	CMO: Generate the right type of demand by driving prospects via signups or free trials, and nurture them with personalized content; engage prospects based on in-product behavioral data.
Chief Revenue Officer (CRO): Prioritize and qualify leads (MQLs and SQLs), and convert them into won deals.	CRO: Prioritize and qualify leads from free trials and signups using product usage and prospect behavior data.
Customer Success Officer (CSO): Onboard, train, renew, upsell, and cross-sell customer.	CSO: Automate customer onboarding and in-product training; determine the right time to ask for renewal, upsell, and cross-sell based on real-time product usage data that correlates with prospect buying intent.

6.5 Key Takeaways

- Customer lifecycle enables companies to focus on the buying process from the customer's point of view rather than from the sales process standpoint.
- Siloed departments make it difficult to design seamless customer experiences.
- Product teams need to be more active in the customer acquisition process and overall customer lifecycle.
- Aggregating customer data across many technologies, managed by different departments, is challenging. Production data and in-product customer behavioral data are essential to creating a unified customer profile view.
- Insufficient customer data is only part of the problem. Companies need tools to create personalized engagement based on timely access to customer data collected across multiple channels.

Here's a quick comparison of old vs. new ways to operate.

Old Way	New Way
Companies separated customer acquisition process across siloed departments, with product teams far removed from the process.	Companies bring product teams closer to the customer acquisition process to design and deliver a seamless customer experience and effective customer engagement.
Customer profile data lived in multiple systems of record that were difficult to centralize and integrate.	Companies find a way to centralize and aggregate customer profile data, including product behavioral and firmographic data.
Customer success teams were primarily responsible for CLV.	Product, marketing, sales, and customer success teams align goals and incentives with CLV.

Chapter 7
From a Traditional Go-To-Market to a Product-led Go-To-Market Strategy

Becoming a customer experience company is a challenging and continuous goal. You can—and should—always improve the customer experience; it's not something you can achieve and put aside. Customer expectations change constantly, and switching cost are low, even in the enterprise markets. That brings us to the core element of the corporate strategy: GTM strategy.

A GTM strategy is similar to a military strategy. It takes into account the following elements:

- The environment and landscape of the battle (i.e., MARKET CONDITIONS) and competitive positioning
- The target or enemy (i.e., TARGET CUSTOMER)
- Weapon of choice (i.e., PRODUCT OFFERING and PRICING)
- How the operation will be carried out (i.e., CUSTOMER ACQUISITION PROCESS and CHANNELS)

Combined, these outline a customer acquisition process, which explains how the company will attract and convert buyers. Here is the definition of a traditional GTM strategy:

> **GTM strategy** is an action plan that describes repeatable and scalable processes for how a company acquires, retains, and grows customers.

So, what impact does GTM strategy have on the quality of customer experience, and why is it crucial for companies to change their GTM strategy if they want to improve customer experience?

As we highlighted, customer experience requires organizations to go beyond demographics and firmographic data to understand customer needs, values, and expectations. These insights will help your organization personalize its product offering, pricing, and message to improve the customer experience; but it will also help you understand what journeys, channels, and processes best match customer expectations. Every organization serious about focusing on customer experience has to evaluate and optimize its GTM strategy to align with a vision of delivering a better customer experience.

It is worth noting that to be successful, a GTM strategy must be repeatable and scalable. Repeatable means that the organization can expect very similar results when executing against a particular GTM playbook. Scalable means the company can hire and train new employees using the GTM playbook, and see proportional revenue growth in acquiring customers.

Traditionally, a GTM strategy highlights channels as the fourth essential element, but in the last two decades, digital transformation drove an explosion of new channels for organizations to reach prospective customers[1]. Seeing that a prospective customer can switch from one channel to another in a matter of seconds, channels themselves became somewhat less important. What matters more is the overall customer acquisition process, which is intertwined with every aspect of a GTM strategy.

In other words, the customer acquisition process is changing because of changing customer expectations and the increasing number of channels through which prospective customers can be reached. Enterprise buyers expect to try and evaluate software in an easy, frictionless way. As a result, a new approach to customer acquisition has emerged where the product itself becomes a channel for acquiring, retaining, and growing customers. This approach fundamentally changes the traditional GTM strategy by elevating product as one of the primary channels. This new strategy is referred to as a product-led GTM strategy. The name suggests the importance of product as a tool and channel to attract, retain, and grow customers.

Product-led go-to-market strategy is an action plan that describes repeatable and scalable processes for how a company acquires, retains, and grows customers, driven by in-product customer behavior, feedback, product usage, and analytics.

In a product-led GTM strategy, the product becomes a crucial and irreplaceable part of every step of how your company prepares to reach and engage prospective customers. In fact, OpenView, a venture capital firm[2], says your product is a key part of your marketing. One of the major benefits of this approach is receiving in-product user behavioral data that can be then used to change or adapt the whole GTM process. How prospective customers interact with your product early in the buying success could help your company make better decisions about what features to build next. You could even adjust marketing messages based on in-product behaviors to highlight values and features that correlate with a higher probability of a prospect becoming a customer. A product-led GTM enables companies to focus more on effective product growth strategies, and incorporate real-time, in-product customer behavioral data to create meaningful engagement across multiple channels and devices.

> Is there anything more relevant and valuable (from a GTM perspective) for a company to improve the customer experience than data showing how prospective customers engage with its product?

> How valuable would it be for you and your extended team to fully understand how and why a single customer (or segment of customers) uses your product, given their unique customer attributes and journeys?

This is a critical point for companies to understand: your product becomes a channel and owned media. We aren't the only ones to note the significance of this shift in the SaaS market: Natalie Diggins, former Entrepreneur in Residence at Openview VP and current VP of Strategy at NeuStar, wrote an article explaining how some companies use their product as a primary growth channel[3].

> How can an organization build an effective GTM strategy without understanding customer behavior, experiences, and journeys within the product?

We hope the answer is clear by now, but let's discuss one other main difference between a traditional and product-led GTM: in the latter, companies focus on driving prospects to try their product instead of driving them to lead forms, and then bombarding them with a bunch of nurturing e-mails. This strategy goes nowhere without prospects filling out lead forms, and one study found[4] that lead forms are filled out on average only 11 percent of the time.

7.1 Are Marketing-Qualified Leads (MQLs) Dead?

Gating content as a way to generate leads has become increasingly less effective. Aside from the fact that prospects do not want to share contact information and would rather evaluate a product via a trial or freemium option, lead forms create inefficiencies in the customer acquisition process. A large portion of leads are prospects that will never be your customers: people who do research on the subject, students, and prospects that don't fit your ideal customer profile.

This fills your database with bad lead data, which can be a big problem. Bad data clutters your marketing automation and CRM solutions with duplicates and bogus data. Depending on how you slice and dice SaaS industry data, the average conversion rate from visitor to lead is around 5 to 15 percent. While the research findings vary, the conversion rate from lead to a won deal is anywhere from 1 to 10 percent. Marketing teams spend a majority of their resources and efforts nurturing leads that are never going to convert. If you still use lead forms and MQLs to generate leads, ask yourself: What percentage of your lead data is garbage (bogus data provided by those filling out your lead forms)? In other words, how much of it is inaccurate data, or from people who aren't truly prospective customers? What percentage of your MQLs fall outside of your ideal customer profile (e.g., two-people startups, students, or maybe even competitors)?

A poor lead conversion rate is partly due to a very low buying intent among prospects that fill out a lead form. On the other hand, signing up for a free trial or freemium product shows a higher interest in your product. Also, a free trial entices prospects to use accurate credentials, since the confirmation process is often a required step for getting meaningful access to the product.

What about lead nurturing and lead scoring? Companies such as Marketo and Hubspot, which popularized a marketing-led customer acquisition approach, also introduced lead scoring and nurturing techniques to help marketers improve conversion rates and bring some kind of prioritization to the process. Lead nurturing based only on contact information (i.e., demographic data) and marketing activities (e.g., opened e-mail, visited web page) can't be very effective. Nurturing and scoring techniques become arbitrary marketing, automating and personalizing interactions with prospects based on data that is only minimally correlated with buying intent. Plus, most organizations cannot personalize e-mail nurturing campaigns, because they lack customer in-product behavioral data.

As a result, companies experience a much-talked-about marketing-sales gap, where marketers pass prospects to sales that aren't ready to buy, and sales complains about lead quality. As an industry, we have to admit that marketing-sales misalignment is due to ineffective lead generation strategies that emphasize quantity of leads over quality. What has made things even more convoluted is that MQLs are not qualified for pipeline forecasting. As a result, sales teams spend time working and further qualifying these leads as SQLs. This not only makes things inefficient, it increases the CAC.

Many teams that made the shift to a product-led GTM strategy have abandoned the traditional approach to customer acquisition and MQLs along with them. If you want to explore this further, read why Tom Wentworth, CMO of RapidMiner, is killing MQLs[5].

Some of the fastest-growing companies in recent years do not put any lead generation forms on their websites, and instead invite prospects to try their products. This list includes Zoom.us, Asana, inVision, and Slack—and it's growing. Prospects search for and find product reviews and other valuable information; after all, they don't want to hear marketing messages that use too much jargon, hyperbole, superlatives, or buzzwords. One quick point on ungated content: Just think about how much marketing attention you are losing by gating your content. When you don't gate your content, readers can share it and contribute to spreading your message across target markets even if they aren't part of your ideal customer profile. But people rarely link or refer to gated content.

Let's be clear: A content strategy around thought leadership is still important for organizations to drive awareness and demand. It has become one of the most efficient ways for companies to engage with prospects, by educating target audiences (prospects and customers) on industry trends, new strategies, and tactics. We believe a sound content strategy is key to growth, but your assets should not hide behind a form. Even more important, your content should be delivered to prospects and customers in a contextual way to move them through the lifecycle.

In an article, Tae Hea Nahm, managing director at Storm Ventures, explains the importance of thought leadership and content strategy for startups[6]. That said, the end goal and metrics will shift from generating marketing leads to driving signups and product-qualified leads (PQLs), in which prospects try the product first.

7.2 What Are Product-Qualified Leads (PQLs)?

One of the earliest mentions of the PQL concept is in an article by Tomasz Tunguz from early 2013, **"THE PRODUCT-QUALIFIED LEAD (PQL)**[7]**."** It describes a natural progression from MQLs to PQLs. However, the PQL only makes sense as part of a larger, product-led GTM strategy.

We believe PQLs are a better way for cross-functional teams to create sales-ready accounts and more active customers. PQLs provide a more accurate method of tracking customer journeys. This is a key metric for any company that's transitioning to a product-led GTM strategy. As a reminder, here's a definition:

Product-qualified lead (PQL) is a prospect that signed up and demonstrated buying intent based on product interest, usage, and behavioral data.

Instead of driving prospects to lead forms, a product-led GTM strategy drives prospects to sign up for a product or free trial. From that moment on, marketing teams can analyze how prospects use the product to nurture or re-engage them until they are ready to buy.

A product-led GTM strategy streamlines the customer acquisition process for SaaS organizations by focusing on one entry point for prospects. When prospective customers sign up for a freemium or free trial, they show a higher buying intent. They also afford the company's teams the opportunity to analyze how prospects interact with the product in their natural environment[8].

Furthermore, marketing teams using behavioral data can re-engage customers that have left the product and haven't returned. Product-led GTM makes it possible for companies to personalize the onboarding experience, and collect insight into what features drive the most value. It also helps pinpoint steps in customer journeys that cause a negative customer experience and result in product abandonment.

Today's sales process rarely incorporates an efficient way for SDRs and AEs to apply product usage data to prioritize their workflow and outreach to prospects. However, sales processes can change in this way when the organization focuses on PQLs instead of MQLs/SQLs. Sales teams can use behavioral data to better prioritize and forecast[9]. Product leaders can get early feedback on what features drive product growth, what in-product journeys are more effective, and what onboarding process results in higher product adoption. Simply put, this approach works for both the company and prospects by enabling a frictionless buying experience.

In the article "WHY PRODUCT-QUALIFIED LEADS ARE THE ANSWER TO A FAILING FREEMIUM MODEL"[10], Christopher O'Donnell explains why PQLs are critical for companies with a freemium business model. However, we believe that product-led GTM strategy and PQLs not only work for the freemium model, but are also essential for almost every SaaS company. Prospects expect to see the product early in the buying process. A product-led strategy brings to life the "don't tell me, let me try!" idea, while PQLs track and measure buying intent more effectively.

To be clear, prospect nurturing and engagement can happen inside the product via in-product messaging, or through other channels such as e-mail, mobile notifications, etc. Customer in-product behavior not only influences how a company nurtures and re-engages customers to come back into the product, but also triggers ideas for content strategy and marketing. Customer behavior is a strong signal of what your target audience cares about, and provides insight into how best to engage with them further.

Let's dive into how a product-led GTM changes the customer acquisition process.

7.3 The Traditional Approach to Customer Acquisition Process

As stated earlier, companies that use the traditional approach to customer acquisition (as shown in Figure 7.1) make it a habit to analyze this process from the company perspective.

What is important to highlight is that a large portion of the traditional customer acquisition process happens outside of the product. This prevents companies from collecting critical behavioral data that can help improve nurturing and customer interaction.

Figure 7.1 - Traditional Acquisition Model

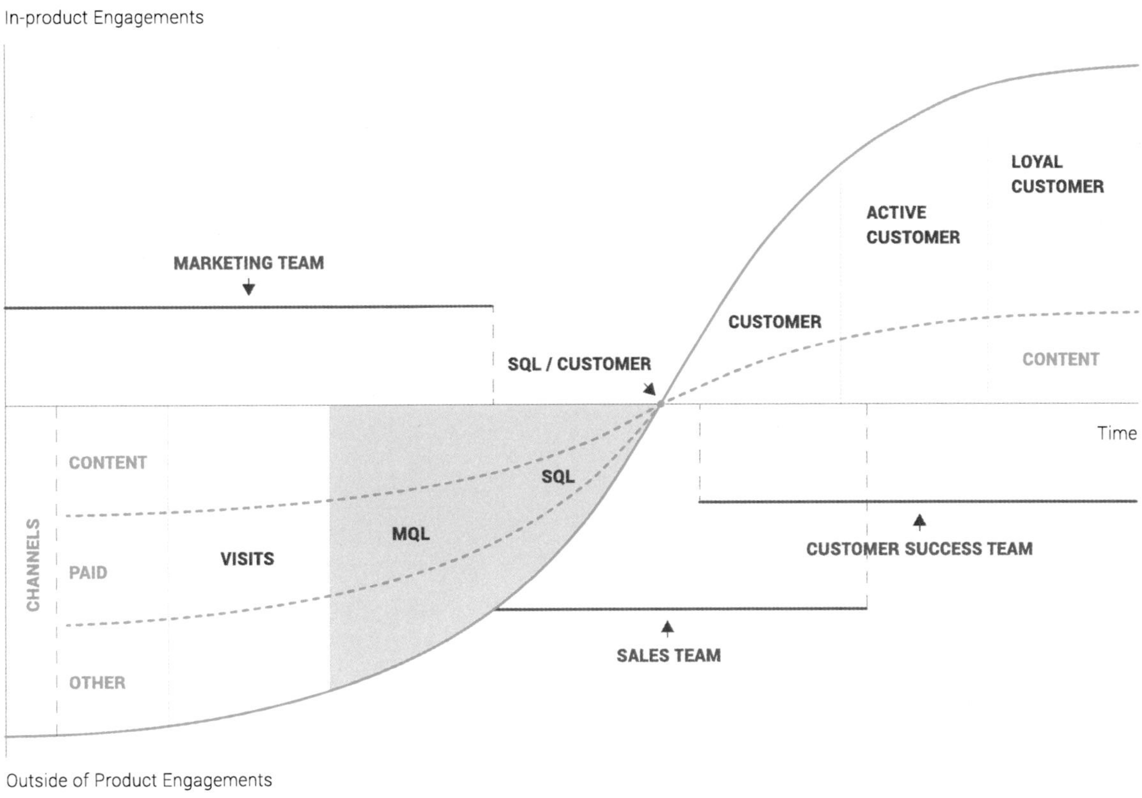

Marketing teams are in charge of the customer lifecycle up until prospects become MQLs. SDRs are responsible for quality marketing leads and generating sales-ready (or sales-qualified) leads (SQLs). AEs focus on converting SQLs into won customers, and then pass them to the customer success team, whose task is to onboard newly acquired customers and ensure they become active and loyal customers. Let's see how a product-led approach changes this process.

7.4 A Product-led Approach to the Customer Acquisition Process

A product-led GTM strategy makes your product an essential part of the acquisition process. Figure 7.2 shows how this strategy significantly reduces the time it takes for prospects to access the product. When compared to the traditional customer acquisition process, companies focus less on the customer lifecycle part outside of product engagement. The customer lifecycle shifts more into the elevated axis area, where product behavior becomes essential in guiding customers through the lifecycle

As explained earlier, product usage data can be leveraged by every team to efficiently move prospects through the customer acquisition process. Furthermore, it is easier for sales, marketing, product, and customer success to agree on what defines a PQL. That's because this metric calls upon more concrete data, compared with the way that MQLs/SQLs are defined.

Figure 7.2 - Product-Led Acquisition Model

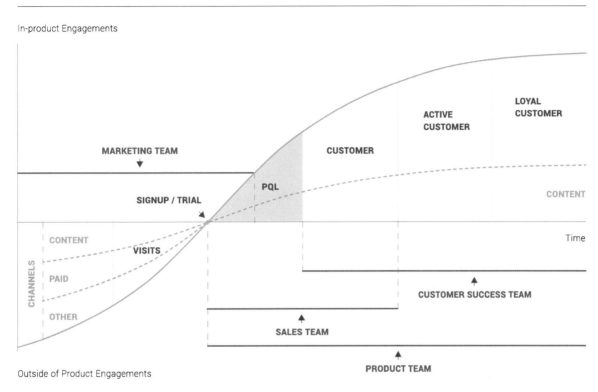

Dropbox is an example of a company that drives prospects directly into the product and nurtures them until they are ready to buy. When prospects approach a certain percent of the storage available on their freemium product, Dropbox sends a notification to the desktop app and over e-mail. It's worth noting that Dropbox has reached a $1B revenue run rate[11] faster than any other company.

As shown, product-led GTM strategies provide several benefits. In a nutshell, product, marketing, sales, and success teams are more aligned to deliver personalized customer experiences that are more engaging and result in higher conversions, loyalty, and revenue growth. By doing this right, companies reduce their CAC, accelerate trial-to-conversions, and increase CLV. In Part III, we dive deep into the essential elements of a product-led GTM strategy.

Old Way	New Way
Companies used traditional GTM strategy.	Companies use product-led GTM strategy driven by product usage and analytics.
Teams focused on MQLs and lead nurturing outside of the product.	Companies drive prospects to use freemium or free trial. then engage and nurture prospects until they're ready to buy.
SDRs and AEs focused on qualification, and closed with limited actionable insight into product usage.	SDRs and AEs streamline process and workflow, driven by insights on how prospects use and engage inside the product.

To deliver great customer experiences today, companies must understand the customer lifecycle, unify customer data, and track their customers' personal journey through their products. This is not possible when following a traditional GTM strategy. However, it is possible when companies embrace a product-led GTM strategy that centers on providing access to the product earlier in the buying cycle via free trials or freemiums.

Such an approach also enables organizations to become truly customer-experience- focused, and provides a clear path for cross-functional teams to align around the buyer's journey and full customer lifecycle. Moreover, it provides the type of product usage insights that are critical for delivering personalized experiences that advance prospects and customers from one stage to the next. These same insights can guide product teams to understand and determine the most valued features and ways to further optimize their products.

Simply put, your product should be at the center of your GTM strategy—your action plan for how your company acquires, retains, and grows customers. To succeed with this approach, every department must align around relevant goals and metrics, and you must equip these teams with the right tools and data.

Part III

Implementing a Product-Led Go-to-Market Strategy

"Ideas are useless unless used The proof of their value is in their implementation. Until then, they are in limbo."

THEODORE LEVITT

Chapter 8
Product-Led Go-To-Market Strategy Overview

Changing customer expectations, along with consumerization of the business buying experience, are ushering in a new customer experience era in SaaS (enterprise software). In Part II, we outlined primary factors that impact how companies can fulfill customer expectations by creating personalized customer experiences. This evolution changes how companies organize and execute their GTM strategy.

We briefly discussed product-led GTM as a new approach to acquire, retain, and grow customers driven by in-product customer behavior, product usage, and analytics. Now let's dig into how to develop a product-led GTM strategy.

As described in the last section, a product-led strategy is an evolution of the GTM strategy. Essentially, a product-led GTM strategy leverages the product as a leading channel through which the company acquires, retains, and grows its customers. It's based on in-product customer behavior, feedback, product usage, and analytics. But what does a product-led GTM strategy entail, and how do you build one?

If you need a refresher on GTM strategy, check out this great presentation by Murray McCaig on the seven-step GTM strategy[1]. McCaig, a venture capitalist and consultant with MaRS, recommends creating a detailed plan for **WHAT** you're selling, **WHO** you're selling to, **HOW** to reach your target market, and **WHERE** you should promote your product. These are the four must-have elements of a GTM strategy. Then, with a strong value proposition, you segment and refine your target market, choose the right channels, and build an effective sales team.

8.1 The Four Essential Elements of a Product-Led GTM Strategy

Developing an effective product-led GTM strategy requires companies to analyze each of the four must-have elements of a GTM strategy by answering these questions:

#1 Customer (WHO)

QUESTIONS:
- Who is your ideal customer?
- What pains do your customers experience?
- Can you describe a day in the life of your target customer?
- How does your product fit into the customer's daily activities and workflow?

OUTCOMES:
- Ideal customer profile (ICP)
- Strategic messaging

#2 Market (WHERE)

QUESTIONS:
- What markets do you want to pursue?
- How big is your addressable market? Is it growing, stable, or declining?
- Who are the biggest players in the market?

OUTCOMES:
- Market segmentation and analysis
- Competitive positioning

#3 Product Offering and Pricing (WHAT)

QUESTIONS:
- What product are you selling? What is your product's unique value proposition?
- How do you describe your product's value?
- How are you different from your competitors?
- What is your product pricing strategy (based on usage, features, capacity, seats, etc.)?
- How do you know which features to build next?

OUTCOMES:
- Product offering
- Value proposition
- Pricing strategy
- Product vision

#4 Channels (HOW)

QUESTIONS:
- What are the most effective channels to reach your target customers?
- What are the most popular publications that your target customers read?
- What social media channels do your customers use the most?
- What channels enable the optimal CAC?
- How do your marketing channels correlate with product signup rates and won deals?

OUTCOMES:
- Demand generation strategy
- Content and distribution strategy
- Paid media strategy
- PR plan

8.2 Setting the Foundation for Your Customer Acquisition Process

The previous four elements come together to form your customer acquisition process. Here are the key questions to answer in regard to this.

QUESTIONS:
- How do you acquire your customers?
- How do you retain and grow your customers?
- What product delivery method should you use (free trials, freemiums, etc.)?
- What details or plays do you need to include in your product, marketing, sales, and customer success playbooks?
- How do you scale your customer acquisition process?
- How do you consistently keep your CLV above CAC? And how can you keep increasing your CLV?

OUTCOMES:
- Business model, including product delivery (freemium, trial, etc.)
- Sales playbook
  - Selling strategies, including positioning and competitive insights
  - Objection handling, prioritization, and forecasting

- Marketing playbook
  - Content and nurturing strategy
  - Customer segmentation
- Customer success playbook
  - Customer onboarding and training
  - Retention and expansion workflows and strategies
- Product playbook
  - Product vision/road map
  - Crucial customer journeys
  - Initial value
  - User onboarding and product adoption metrics

Figure 8.1 – Product-Led GTM

For the early stage startup, the first milestone in executing a GTM strategy is reaching **PRODUCT/ MARKET FIT**. Essentially, product/market fit is an experimen-tation process of finding customers in a target market with a problem that your product can address, for a price (or total cost of ownership) below the level of value that's provided in exchange.

A lot has been written about product/market fit, so we won't spend much time going over it here.

We suggest reading "**12 THINGS ABOUT PRODUCT-MARKET FIT**[2]" by Tren Griffin, and **"PRODUCT/ MARKET FIT: WHAT IT REALLY MEANS, HOW TO MEASURE IT, AND WHERE TO FIND IT"**[3] by Eric Jorgenson, for more detailed overviews.

A broader but related concept, **COMPANY/MARKET FIT**, may be more relevant, since it combines **PAIN-PRODUCT FIT** and **CUSTOMER-MESSAGE FIT** ideas. You can find a more detailed overview in Part 1 of How to Develop Strategic Messaging and Positioning[4].

In the early stages of GTM, finding product/market fit is critical, while a scalable, repeatable customer acquisition process is less so. However, after you find the perfect product/market fit, you should focus on optimizing your customer acquisition process to reach ideal customers in a scalable, repeatable, and profitable way.

We recently spoke with Tae Hea Nahm, co-founder and managing director at Storm Ventures, and he underscored the importance of this last point. In his experience, the main reason startups with a product/market fit fail to accelerate growth is due to lack of a repeatable and scalable GTM strategy. Companies that find an effective (i.e., repeatable and scalable) way to acquire customers— what Tae Hea Nahm refers to as "GTM fit"—can increase and better forecast revenue growth as they invest more in their GTM strategy and headcount.

While a product-led approach impacts every part of a GTM strategy, it has a transformational effect on the customer acquisition process. Note: a product-led GTM strategy, as an evolution of a traditional GTM strategy, can be applied to new product launches as well as to existing products.

The consistent user feedback generated through a product-led strategy enables companies to make meaningful changes to the customer acquisition process, as well as to their product. Organizations can optimize marketing campaigns, sales processes, and run product growth experiments.

All four aspects of a GTM strategy—customer, market, product, and channels—are influenced by a product-led approach.

It's critical to go through the product-led GTM strategy exercise we described before launching your product (i.e., during the pre-product stage). It's also essential to embrace the idea of a continuous process of testing and optimizing the customer acquisition process after the product is released.

Teams can conduct external customer surveys and interviews to gather quantitative and qualitative data, but this feedback is less reliable than real-time behavioral data showing how customers use and respond to a product. There is no substitute for in-product user behaviors, because this data provides deep insight into how customers use and value your product (as opposed to how they say they value it).

Furthermore, this data enables the company to learn about the user and guide that person to explore the full spectrum of product features and capabilities, or the most relevant and useful.

Chapter 9
Driving Customer Acquisition and Adoption with a Product-Led Strategy

Now let's explore how a product-led GTM strategy affects the four major phases of the customer lifecycle: acquisition, adoption, retention, and expansion. First, we will explore the initial phases (acquisition and adoption), and then we will dive into the follow-on phases (retention and expansion).

9.1 The Four Steps to Leading with a Product-Led Strategy

What we have covered so far may feel theoretical or daunting, so in this chapter, we are getting down into the nuts and bolts of putting a product-led strategy into place.

Step 1: Drive prospects to try the product

A product-led GTM strategy aligns teams—and more specifically, marketing—to zero in on one call to action (CTA), such as a "Free Trial" or "Signup" for a freemium. This helps everyone—but marketing in particular—focus on getting prospects through one valuable conversion door.

The product-led strategy doesn't change the goal of marketing to generate demand through a variety of channels, using quality thought leadership content and other means. However, two shifts occur that make marketing teams more efficient and effective at building awareness and acquiring customers.

First, marketing uses a single CTA, where the signup page becomes a personalized landing page, so instead of creating multiple landing pages and lead forms, as was the case in the MQLs era, marketing can use a product signup page as a landing page for testing and optimizing conversions.

Second, a product-led approach provides marketing teams with a new dimension of data: product usage. They can, in turn, use this to develop and offer higher-quality thought leadership content and build marketing campaigns focused on profitable customer segments with a higher potential CLV.

Here is an example of this at work. Let's take PandaDoc, a company providing a document management solution that helps companies create, send, and track proposals and quotes. Because the company tracks and analyzes a large number of quotes and proposals, it can provide insights into how to improve response time and accuracy. For example, PandaDoc found that shorter proposals, sent earlier in the day, with a deadline attached, are signed faster. In its content, PandaDoc shares insights such as these that it has learned by studying how its product is used. In this way, its product-led approach empowers it to create thought leadership content that helps its prospects and customers learn how to be more effective. In other words, understanding how customers use your product can directly impact your content strategy and marketing campaigns.

A lot of guesswork is eliminated from the process of creating marketing campaigns because teams analyze profitable customer segments through product usage and target those segments.

Step 2: Design your free trial process or freemium offer

The two most popular pricing models in SaaS are freemium and free trials. Let's finally define freemium and free trial strategies:

> **Freemium** is a customer acquisition model that provides access to part of a software product to prospects free of charge, without a time limit.

> **Free trial** is a customer acquisition model that provides a partial or complete product to prospects free of charge for a limited time. Typically, a free trial runs for 14 or 30 days.

There are pros and cons to both approaches. Some companies don't support a freemium strategy because it can create additional costs for the organization to serve free customers, but many companies find it effective. Remember: A freemium product does not limit the amount of time a prospect can access the software, but often limits users in some way, such as through stripped-back features or allowed amount of usage. Slack employs a freemium model, and so do Zoom.us, Dropbox, and Asana. Companies such as Atlassian, Github, and Twilio focused on the developer market, and started with freemium.

When deciding whether a free trial or freemium strategy is right for your company and product, we recommend estimating the size of the addressable market. Jason Lemkin outlines the math behind making freemium work in his article "WHY YOU NEED 50 MILLION ACTIVE USERS FOR FREEMIUM TO ACTUALLY WORK". Suffice to say, the addressable market should be large enough for you to capture a significant chunk of it and be profitable while only converting 10 percent of free users. The pros and cons of freemium and free trial are highlighted in Table 9.1.

Table 9.1 - Pros and Cons of Freemium and Free Trial

Freemium	Free Trial
Pros/Opportunities	
• Puts your product in front of more people early in their decision-making process. • Potentially undercuts your competitors, and repositions your company and product in the marketplace. • Collects product-related data and aggregate product data; can even provide insights into industry standards—for example, average time to sign a contract (see PandaDoc example above).	• Prospects who "stick it out" and go through the sign-up and trial process tend to be more serious about the product that you're offering. • In a short time frame, trial users invest a good amount of time and effort trying your product, and if their experience is good, they stay with you. Time is valuable, and if your solution works, that may be the end of their search. • The user gets the full product experience and can test their usage of your product in a "real-life" situation, allowing them to easily understand how the product can impact their business. • The time limit on free trials can create a sense of urgency to use the product.
Cons/Risks	
• The cost to serve free customers (who never upgrade) must be balanced with enough paying customers to enable a sustainable business. • Product gets positioned in the prospect's mind from the perspective of a scaled down version. To prompt users to sign up for the paid version, companies must hold back features. This can create an inferior user experience and fail to convey the full value of the product.	• Limited product exposure limits virality and buzz. • Bigger initial investment: in order to take advantage of a free trial, users typically have to provide more information about themselves than with a freemium offer. Anything that stands between prospects and the product (such as requesting lots of information during sign-up) will cause some users to disengage.

Freemium model considerations

There are many ways to structure a freemium offering, including feature-limited, capacity-limited, seat-limited, customer-class-limited, support-limited, and time- or bandwidth-limited. Lincoln Murphy's[2] article provides a good overview of seven types of freemium to consider.

Here are questions for your team to ask when considering a freemium model:

- How much will it cost to sustain a large segment of free customers?
  Is a freemium model scalable for your business?
- Can we provide enough value for users to realize product benefits but still limit value to entice them to pay for a subscription?
- How difficult is it to get started with the product? Does it require technical integration and broader organizational approval?
- How will we nurture and prioritize freemium users that are ready to purchase?
- Are we attracting the right kind of customer (i.e., a customer in our target market with a real need, an urgency to purchas,e and a desire to expand the subscription)?

To recap, freemium makes more sense when your organization is facing:

- A large addressable market
- Low costs to serve free users
- Low barriers/commitment for users to start with your product

If your company meets these criteria, freemium may be the way to go. Note: Make sure you articulate how different the user experience is between free and paid versions; prospects need to know what they're missing.

Consider a free trial strategy before making a choice.

Free trial considerations

The goal of the free trial is to deliver as much value as possible to users during their trial period. For the purpose of this discussion, we will concentrate on an ungated free trial strategy, which means a user can sign up and set up a trial without talking to a sales rep. With gated free trials, users request access to the product and get approved by a sales or sales development representative. An ungated free trial is essentially a self-service version of the traditional Proof of Concept (PoC) approach.

Important questions to consider before deciding whether a free trial strategy is right for your organization:

- How long does it take for prospects to realize initial value on average?
  How long should the trial last?
- What features can and should our team limit or remove from the free trial process?
- How do we nurture a free-trial user? What in-product behavior correlates with
  an optimal trial-to-customer conversion rate?

A free trial signup process is typically the first time prospects come into contact with your product. An effective trial signup includes a simple, guided journey that is painless and immediate. The critical part of the guided journey is getting prospects to an "A-ha!" moment, when they experience and realize the true value of your product.

Think of a free trial as a chance for users to test drive your product like they would a new car, on their own, seeing how it handles when driven to their favorite or most-visited places. Picture them taking it on a winding back road and pushing it on the freeway. There's no salesman with these prospects, but the guide makes sure the journey takes them where they need to go to experience the right "A-ha!" moment.

Table 9.2 outlines important considerations for launching a successful free trial process, and shows how it maps to our own software trial process.

Table 9.2 - Design Considerations for Free Trial Experiences

	Considerations	Aptrinsic Example
Goal	• What goals do you want prospects to achieve during free trials? • What value do you want to deliver to prospects? • What valued features do you want prospects to try? • What are the requirements for prospects to become PQLs? • Do you provide a self-service option to buy at the end of the trial?	• Send first engagement campaign
Type	• What type of free trial do you offer? Do you limit your free trial in any way?	• Full product features/capabilities • Usage-based limitation
Features	• What features do you want to offer and/or limit during free trial? • What are the valued features that you want to offer?	• Install JS tracking • Create, send first engagement • Create customer segment
Duration	• How long should the free trial last? • When and why should you extend the free trial duration?	• 14-day trial • 30-day trial
Buyer Personas	• Do you expect that only end users will sign up for a free trial? • Does it make sense to differentiate between influencers, decision makers, and end users during a free trial? • If so, how do your signup process, journey to experience initial value, and nurturing efforts change?	• Targets end user • Invite another buying persona
Signup Process & Requirements	• What is your signup process for a free trial? • What information do you request from prospects? • How many steps are in your free trial setup? • What is required from prospects to access a free trial (such as corporate e-mail, credit card, social login, third-party integration information)?	• Ask for e-mail (corporate e-mail required) • Confirm e-mail • No credit card required • Product tutorial

	Considerations	Aptrinsic Example
Customer Journey to Initial Value	• What are the steps in the buyer/customer journey to experience initial value or the desired outcome? • What is considered initial value?	• Signup • Create and send first engagement • Create customer segment • Build the first onboarding experience
Usage (Frequency)	• How often do you want prospects to log in and use your product during the trial period? • Can your product become a part of their daily routine?	• Send daily suggestions on what customer segments to act on.
Nurturing	• How will you communicate with prospects during the trial (e-mails, in-product messages, etc.)? • What content would be helpful for prospects to review before or during their free trial?	• Number of nurturing e-mails (frequency) • Triggers for in-product messages • Set up in-product onboarding sequences and guided product tours
Metrics	• What metrics do you want to measure during a free trial? • What in-product user behavior do you want to track? • How will you measure and report signup-to-PQL and signup-to-customer conversion rates? • What customer segments and roles correlate with shorter time to PQLs and closed deals?	• Number of signups • Number of PQLs • Signup-to-PQL conversion rate
Cost of Free Trial	• What is needed, and how much will it cost your company, to offer a free trial? • How do your CAC and free trial costs align with your PQL goals?	• Cloud storage • Real-time analytics services • Bandwidth

Let's dig a bit deeper into how a product-led approach enables and impacts these various design considerations.

Personalizing the experience

A product-led GTM strategy empowers product, marketing, sales, and success teams to think of their products as marketing and sales channels. In fact, any part of the free trial experience can be personalized. Not only can the product be personalized, but so can the customer acquisition experience—through the free trial, pricing, messaging, and contextual engagement. Let's go over some of these in more detail.

Initial signup process considerations

The free trial signup is basically your product signup process, and it's critical for your teams to spend time thinking about the complexity, clarity, and user experience. Minimizing the amount of information required for prospects to sign up, and reducing the number of steps in the signup process, are easy ways to improve the experience from the start.

> TIP: Design a signup process that only highlights one action per step. Avoid asking for personal or contact information that is not essential to get started with your product, unless it increases the value your product can deliver. Also, track the steps in the process so you can pinpoint where prospects fall off and become inactive.

Initial value and customer journey considerations

Prospects who sign up for your free trials should experience initial value (or a desired outcome), ideally in an experience that doesn't turn them off. Put another way, you want prospects to start using your product with as little friction as possible. That's means don't ask about company size, job title, revenue, industry, or credit card information as a signup requirement.

Next, you must enable them to accomplish their goal as easily as possible to reach the initial value. Kintan Brahmbhatt, Director of Product Management at Amazon, describes this as getting them to "perform one meaningful task...that sets expectations for a future engagement."[3]

To reach initial value, prospects need to go through a core journey that represents a set of actions leading to desired value. In Part III, we provided a few examples of how some well-known companies track journeys on the way to initial value. Zoom.us, for example, orchestrates a smooth experience for new users to sign up, organize, and hold their first video conferences.

> TIP: Design the shortest and most meaningful journey for prospects to experience initial value.

Free trial duration and usage frequency considerations

Regardless of free trial duration, your company doesn't need to wait until the end of the trial period to try to convert prospects. Trial duration provides urgency for prospects to take action. But whenever a prospect realizes initial value and reaches PQL status, this signals a good time for your sales team to engage in a buying conversation.

The goal of every SaaS product is to become an essential part of the prospect's daily life and workflow. The more often prospects engage with your product's core capabilities, the more likely they are to convert. With that in mind, monitor how frequently prospects log in to your product during the free trial. Prospects are more likely to create new habits (such as accomplishing a daily task a certain way) the more frequently they use your product.

> TIP: Don't wait until the end of the trial period to engage with a prospect. Show how your product fits into their daily activities, routine, and workflow.

Free trials and a new wave of growth-hacking

Free trials can support personalized growth strategies, such as extending a free trial if a prospect completes a certain number of actions or invites more team members to participate. One reason to extend a free trial is to engage multiple end-users as well as different buying personas in the organization—to build a team habit that could lead to a higher selling price.

For example, your company can design and test a few different ways of inviting team members, or allowing prospects to extend the trial invitation to people in their extended networks. The incentives could be to increase free trial duration or increase product usage. A few companies in the cloud space, including Dropbox, incentivize with increased storage space, but it could be a much smaller action that incentivizes usage. Perhaps you make it easy for a prospect to send a pre-composed Tweet or other social media share once they've successfully onboarded or reached the end of a successful use-case journey. For example, Unroll.me, a service that helps you instantly unsubscribe from unwanted e-mail subscriptions and clean your e-mail inbox, asks users to share about their experience on Twitter and Facebook.

Bottom line: A product-led approach empowers your teams to experiment with growth-hacking strategies designed to increase awareness, virality, signups, and prospect conversions.

> TIP: Explore opportunities to extend free trials based on certain prospect behaviors; target to increase account penetration (more peers exposed to the product) and to increase signups from other organizations and individuals.

Product demos during free trials

In a traditional sense, the "Request a Demo" CTA was part of the MQL generation process. The idea was to qualify prospects and show them a targeted and personalized product demo. With a product-led GTM strategy, a product demo can be a supplemental engagement targeted to prospects while they are in free trials.

In-product behavioral data helps your teams understand where and how a prospect is struggling with learning about and using your product. If your organization can create pre-packaged, yet personalized, training sessions addressing the most common roadblocks, you could show these to users during their free trial when relevant.

For more complex software solutions, a free trial can be a trigger to send a prospect an e-mail or in-product message with a product demo offer. This could be a great opportunity for your sales team to engage with prospects in more meaningful ways. In this case, your sales team's role is to help prospects learn your product, rather than just push the sale. This consultative approach to selling becomes more effective with a product-led strategy, because your sales team can better prepare for product demos based on prospect in-product behavior.

> TIP: Offer prospects a free trial, and then a personalized demo, if your product is more complex or requires more effort to set up and onboard.

Measuring free trial success

Measuring the effectiveness of a free trial is necessary for optimization and experimentation purposes. These are common metrics for measuring success:

- Number of trial signups, PQLs, and closed deals
- Average time from signup to PQL (time to initial value)
- Trial-to-PQL conversion rate
- Average engagement based on features and timeframe
- Frequencies of login (daily, times/week)
- Number of prospects per account

We will cover metrics in more detail later in section 4.6.

> TIP: Analyze prospects' behaviors during free trials and identify key triggers that cause them to move along their journeys toward realizing initial value.

Step 3: Create onboarding experiences

Often prospect (or user) onboarding and customer onboarding terms are used interchangeably. However, from the perspective of a product-led GTM strategy, it makes sense to differentiate between prospect and customer onboarding, because these users have different goals and are at different stages of the customer lifecycle.

> **Prospect (or user) onboarding** is how a prospect moves through initial signup, experiences initial value, and reaches PQL status. It is designed to help users become familiar with the product and realize initial value as soon as possible.
>
> **Customer onboarding** is the process of getting a newly subscribed customer (or account) up and running effectively with your product, which usually includes much guidance and hand-holding. The goal here is to set the customer up to realize the full value of your product, thereby retaining customers while also expanding business within the account, or getting referrals from your happy customers.

There are practical reasons to differentiate user and customer onboarding. Customer onboarding includes in-depth product training, setting up individual users for the account, guiding customers through third-party integrations, setting up payments, and periodic check-ins. This is especially true for more technical products requiring high-touch sales.

Figure 9.1 - User Onboarding vs. Customer Onboarding

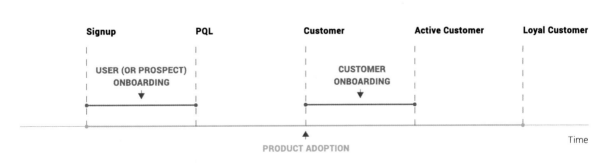

Even though we differentiate prospect and customer onboarding, the onboarding process itself is a continuous process. As soon as a prospect is onboarded and becomes a customer, customer onboarding begins. Assuming you continually introduce new features, customer onboarding doesn't ever stop, as the process needs to be repeated to encourage the adoption of new product capabilities.

That said, onboarding morphs into the adoption process, and adoption never ends. The onboarding process has specific milestones and goals, while adoption is a continuous process. In this regard, we slightly disagree with Intercom[4] —just as you can't continuously board a plane, you can't continuously onboard, because once you have onboarded, you begin the (continuous) process of adoption.

Ideally, a person will onboard twice—first as a user, and then as a customer—but then they move into the adoption process. Just as it's a never-ending process to hone your skills at something (say, skiing), it's a never-ending process to adopt and make the best use of a product and new features.

How Aptrinsic onboards prospects
Figure 9.2 outlines how we at Aptrinsic think about onboarding our prospects and customers.

Figure 9.2 - User (Prospect) Onboarding (Aptrinsic example)

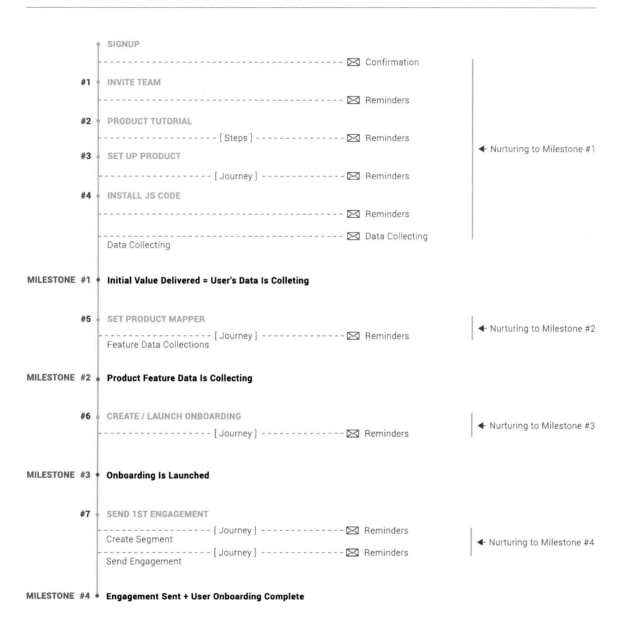

Let's take a closer look at our onboarding process.

Phase 1: Reaching initial value

Steps 1 through 4, in Figure 9.2, show the customer journey to initial value. Prospects experience initial value when they install our JS code and start collecting user data.

MILESTONE #1: Install JS code and start collecting data

NOTE: Each step could contain smaller sub-journeys. For example, Step #3 — Set Up Product— will include multiple interactions.

Phase 2: Setting up Aptrinsic Product Mapper™

In step 5, we outline the journey that a prospect takes to start collecting data on specific product features and interactions.

MILESTONE #2: Collecting usage data for specific product features + becoming PQL

Phase 3: Designing onboarding experience

In step 6, we guide prospects to create and launch onboarding guides for their users.

MILESTONE #3: Prospect launches onboarding experience for customers

Phase 4: Sending first campaign

In step 7, prospects are guided to create their first customer segment and first engagement campaign.

MILESTONE #4: Prospect's onboarding is complete

We organized our onboarding experience into four phases and defined milestones for each. The order of these phases can change, but for prospects to understand the value of our product, they have to complete all four phases.

Our onboarding process may look similar to others, but a couple of notable distinctions make this a product-led approach. First, we base our nurturing campaigns on in-product behaviors. Second, we clearly define a PQL as a prospect who completes milestones one and two (installed JS and set up our Product Mapper).

As soon as a prospect reaches PQL status, our SDR is notified to follow up with the prospect to offer a personalized demo of the full product.

How to Ensure a Successful Prospect Onboarding Experience

Here are nine things you should always do when onboarding prospects.

1. Define onboarding goals and milestones
To know when a prospect is onboarded, define exactly what it means to be onboarded.

> What set of actions must prospects complete to realize the full value of our product?

Connecting onboarding goals with milestones enables your teams to know where prospects fall off and why. Additionally, every milestone should end with a prospect receiving new value from your product. Hitting a milestone should feel like a completed task. Let's take a closer look at how we design onboarding goals and milestones at Aptrinsic.

Aptrinsic example:

GOAL: Prospect (account) launches first onboarding experience for its customers and sends first engagement campaign.

MILESTONES:

1   INSTALLS JS CODE
a   Invites team
b   Completes product tutorial
c   Creates product
d   Installs JS code

CUSTOMER VALUE: Prospect can see their users' activity data from product usage.

2   SETS UP PRODUCT MAPPER
CUSTOMER VALUE: Prospect can now itemize product features.

3   LAUNCHES FIRST ONBOARDING CAMPAIGN
CUSTOMER VALUE: Prospect can see how new onboarding experiences unfold.

4   SENDS FIRST ENGAGEMENT CAMPAIGN

a   Creates customer segment
b   Designs engagement campaign for the segment

CUSTOMER VALUE: Prospect monitors how new engagement brings the user back into the product.

2. Simplify customer journeys

To reach each milestone, a prospect completes a set of actions that resembles a journey. It's important to simplify these journeys and ensure that nothing distracts prospects from achieving their goal with the product.

Teams can improve the onboarding success by focusing on one action a prospect needs to complete per step. Minimizing the number of options helps prevent decision paralysis and dissatisfaction.

To recap, customer journeys should:
- Include one action per step
- Be limited to 5-7 steps to complete a milestone
- Guide prospects with personal and simple messages

InVision is a great example of a simple onboarding experience. You can sign up on their website for a free trial, and in just five steps, you're ready to create your first project. Each step in the InVision onboarding journey is focused on a single action. All other distractions are eliminated.

3. Get to initial value quickly

When prospects sign up for a freemium or free trial, they want to address certain pains or needs. It's best to focus on understanding what constitutes initial value for them, and reducing the time to realize that value.

For example, InVision's five-step initial signup process doesn't ask for things that aren't necessary such as uploading an image for your avatar or connecting to social media sites. These actions don't help prospects reach their initial value and understanding of the product, so it's wise not to include them in onboarding.

4. Address "zero data/empty state"

"Zero data" or "empty state" is what prospects see during their initial signup process when no data is available in the product. The way to address this issue is to guide the prospect through a journey that populates, uploads, or integrates data into your product. Benjamin Brandall, in his article "**THE MOST OVERLOOKED ASPECT OF UX DESIGN COULD BE THE MOST IMPORTANT**"[5], argues that empty state is a great opportunity for teams to highlight emotional connections with users. Empty state can entice users with one CTA that will help make your app experience more meaningful. You might get inspired by the 40 clever empty state designs for mobile apps shared in this article by Nancy Young[6].

5. Define a PQL

In the world of marketing automation, lead scoring is the primary method that marketing teams use to monitor how prospects are nurtured and determine the right moment for SDR teams to qualify prospects. With a product-led strategy, a PQL serves this purpose. It is essentially an activated user that has realized initial value within your SaaS product, and is showing enough interest to trigger your sales team to engage with that prospective customer.

While the definition of a PQL remains consistent from company to company, each organization must determine their formula for determining a PQL. For example, at Aptrinsic, a PQL is a prospect that completes Milestone 1 + Milestone 2. The most effective way to determine your formula is to get your marketing, sales, customer success, and product teams together to collaborate on an agreed-upon definition.

Aptrinsic PQL = install JS code (MILESTONE 1) **+ set up Product Mapper** (MILESTONE 2)

6. Personalize the onboarding experience with custom journeys

If inviting a prospect's team members into the trial is part of your onboarding process, you've got an amazing opportunity to design and test personalized experiences based on buyer or user roles. For example, at Aptrinsic, we guide end-users to create a segment or campaign. But we believe it is more valuable to guide Chief Product Officers to their dashboard and walk them through each metric.

> Does your prospect or customer onboarding experience change depending on the buyer persona?

Setup wizards, product tours and tutorials, walkthroughs, and tool tips are examples of ways to design personalized onboarding experiences. Their capabilities and functionality vary, but they are intended to help prospects and customers adopt your product.

For example, a progress bar and checklist can show prospects where they are in the product setup process. Many enterprise software products also include a notification center as a central location for all important communications and updates. This enables companies to personalize communication with prospects and guide them to the next onboarding step, all within the product.

7. Nurture with personalized communication

An onboarding experience can take a prospect an hour, a week, or even a few months. That said, personalized communication can accelerate the process. E-mail and in-product messages are two primary channels to re-engage and guide prospects when they abandon onboarding journeys.

> TIP: In-product messages are effective for influencing customers to engage in specific ways, because they're already in the product.

You can configure e-mails to be triggered to send automatically based on a prospect's action or inaction, reminding them about product value and driving them back into the product with a single CTA.

Other examples of action-based (or time-based) communication triggered by a specific action or inaction include welcome e-mails and notifications that the app started collecting data or that a team member joined the product. Here is an example of a time-based trigger: a prospect leaves without completing the journey to initial value, and within 24 hours receives an e-mail reminder encouraging a return to the product to complete the journey.

In addition, you can call upon transactional communications to nurture prospects. Examples include confirmation e-mails, "reset your password" e-mails, copies of the receipt, and so on.

When using nurture:

- Behavior-based (or action-based) communication works best
- Time-based triggers help engage at the right time and in the right channel
- Transactional and behavior-based communication can be delivered with e-mail or in-product messaging

8. Document important customer journeys

Tutorials, walkthroughs, and tool tips are effective for guiding prospects within the product, but remember to provide clear documentation that breaks down a specific journey or use case to support in-product engagement.

During the onboarding process, prospects may complete a product tour or a walk-through, but over time they will likely forget how to accomplish a task and turn to documentation, which can guide them step by step. Detailed documentation can even assist prospects in evaluating the core values and ease of using your product. Asana provides an example of clear and helpful documentation in its resource center[7].

9. Measure and track prospects through onboarding

When it comes to tracking the onboarding experience, you must focus on these two aspects:

- Understanding where prospects fall off (abandon the journey)
- Understanding the velocity at which prospects move through milestones

In-depth product analytics enable your teams to understand where prospects leave their journeys, and how best to tune nurturing communications to address these issues. In some cases, product analytics will inform teams about the need to redesign certain steps—or the whole journey—to improve the percentage of successfully onboarded prospects.

For tracking, consider:

- Number of prospects signed up
- Number of prospects that started vs. number who completed journeys and milestones
- How prospects complete each step in the journey

To recap, here are the nine steps:

1. Define onboarding goals and milestones
2. Simplify customer journeys
3. Get to initial value quickly
4. Address "zero data/empty state"
5. Define a PQL
6. Personalize the onboarding experience with custom journeys
7. Nurture with personalized communication
8. Document important customer journeys
9. Measure and track prospects through onboarding

IMPORTANT NOTE: The initial signup and prospect onboarding experience is a critical step in moving users through the customer lifecycle—delivering initial value, reaching PQL, and so on. Customer adoption and retention begins as soon as a prospect starts the signup process. Every milestone on the road to reaching onboarding success has to deliver a valuable outcome. The onboarding experience is not something to be overlooked. It's a critical aspect of making your prospects understand the ins and outs of your product and its value. By carefully and continuously analyzing the onboarding experience, your teams will understand how effective the process is and how to improve it.

Step 4: Reaching PQLs and converting to customers

As prospects progress through the customer lifecycle, you want them to reach two important milestones. First, newly signed prospects should reach PQL status. Second, you want them to quickly convert from PQL to a closed deal.

It's a mistake to think about this in a vacuum, as it only pertains to your product. When making buying decisions, prospects are often deciding between four options:

1. Use your product
2. Do it themselves
3. Don't do it all
4. Use your competitor's product

To accelerate the sales process, your teams should find the best way to show how your product provides more or higher-value benefits when compared to the other options. Doing so—and moving prospects through the acquisition stage—means addressing the common reasons why prospects choose not to buy:

1. Lacks a clear understanding of your product's value
2. Has the wrong perception of the product's functionality
3. Doesn't know how to use your product
4. Wasn't onboarded quickly enough or wasn't re-engaged at the right time
   - Doesn't experience pain often enough to frequently use your product
   - Requires features that are not part of your product
5. Lacks budget
6. Their tech stack doesn't integrate well with your product

Now, let's look closely at other tactics that teams can use to accelerate their sales cycles.

Prioritize prospects and PQLs based on in-product behaviors

Prospects expect sales teams to be more knowledgeable about them, their needs, and industry practices. Companies can become more agile by prioritizing efforts based on how engaged prospects are with their products. Here are examples of this in action:

- Behavioral data can help sales teams create more relevant calls with prospects
- A product-led strategy supports a more accurate prediction of which prospect has the highest trial-to-close conversion rate and CLV
- The longer a company uses a product-led strategy, the more accurate cross-functional teams get at identifying customer segments with a higher probability to renew and upgrade

Automate self-service checkout for low-touch customer segments

Sometimes, companies assume that interaction with a prospect customer prior to the sale is always a good thing. But in many instances, prospects prefer a better customer experience to complete their buying process without any contact with sales. In fact, studies show that 47 percent of Baby Boomers prefer self-service, while a whopping 64 percent of millennials do too[8]. We anticipate that a larger portion of business buyers will expect self-service options going forward.

If your product has a broad addressable market, you can capitalize on this trend—and stop wasting valuable sales resources—by offering self-service checkout for a low-touch customer segment can accelerate prospect conversion. Instead of investing in sales resources to convert prospects with a low average selling price (ASP), you can guide low-touch prospects to self-service journeys.

Automate just-in-time personalized engagements

Action-based and time-based engagements can automate some qualification steps that were traditionally part of an SDR process. For example, you can create in-product messages and communications as well as emails to influence prospects to get back into the product and move toward a PQL conversion. This frees SDRs to focus on helping prospects and customers with more personalized services, such as custom product demos.

Organize your teams to target the best accounts

In a traditional GTM approach, marketing and sales build custom campaigns targeting specific accounts based on potential ASP and CLV. With a product-led approach, cross-functional teams identify profitable customer segments among prospects in free trials, and design campaigns to target these accounts through social media and advertising channels. Retargeting meaningful personas in the accounts that are in the free trial process enables more efficient spending and higher ROI.

Vision is important for business buyers. That's why successful companies find a way to communicate product road maps at the closing stage of the buying process. In many cases, a vision will help your team close a deal.

Deliver thought leadership content at every stage of the customer lifecycle

In order to accelerate the sales cycle, cross-functional teams need to understand all personas involved in the buying process. Each persona has a different concern, objection, and perception. One way to engage various personas is with thought leadership content that addresses their individual priorities as well as team-based needs around common concerns and goals.

Traditionally, thought leadership content is delivered at the very top of the funnel, to boost awareness. We understand that thought leadership content is usually reserved for exploring issues and trends and provoking potential customers to consider a new perspective. That said, we believe thought leadership can—and should—be used to characterize content quality rather than content type (or the stage at which it should be used).

We agree that certain content will never qualify as thought leadership; but there's no reason companies can't present webinars and guides that teach late-stage customers new and more effective workflows, strategies, or tactics. A product-led strategy makes it easier to deliver this type of content because it provides direct insight how users behave in the product. By drawing upon these insights, organizations can offer quality educational content to assist prospects and customers at every stage of the lifecycle. Whether or not you refer to this as thought leadership, the outcome is the same: deliver value that sets the organization apart and helps drive more revenues.

Remember: with a product-led GTM strategy, your product becomes the primary driver of customer acquisition, retention, and growth. That means you must invest more time and money creating content that helps users learn the product, including product documentation, how-to guides, industry benchmarks, and so on. Content plays an active role in getting people to use your product, so keeping your documentation in good shape is as important as publishing engaging articles to engage new prospects.

Create targeted product demos for trial/freemium customers

In the MQL era, the "request a demo" CTA was used to generate leads and enable sales teams to show the product to a prospect for the first time. With a product-led strategy, you can drive prospects to PQLs, or conversion events to prospects already familiar with your product enables teams to accelerate the sales cycles by testing buying intent. Specifically, your company can design in-product CTAs and offer guided product demos that reveal prospects' buying intentions and even trigger movement through the lifecycle drive. For example, let's say your prospect realizes initial value via a free trial, but has not reached PQL status. Your team can offer a sales-guided product demo with an in-product CTA. If the prospect responds to the CTA, you can accelerate their conversion to a PQL.

All the strategies described above in Step 4 impact at least one of the following goals:

* Reduce the time it takes from trial to PQL and from PQL to close
* Increase the Trial-to-PQL rate and PQL-to-Customer rate
* Increase average CLV by focusing on the right accounts

Simply put, a product-led GTM strategy enables cross-functional teams to increase the velocity from the time prospects become familiar with the company and product to the time they buy. In addition, it can potentially increase revenues by letting sales and marketing focus on profitable customer segments and activities.

9.2 Key Takeaways

* Convince prospects to try the product with a single CTA, such as a product signup page.
* Understand the advantages and disadvantages to freemiums and free trials, and choose the one that works best for your company:
    * Freemium is best with a large addressable market, low costs of serving free users, and low barriers to start
    * Free trial is best if it can deliver or highlight as much product value as possible in a limited time
* Any part of a free trial can be personalized, including initial signup, initial value, and customer journey considerations, such as trial duration and usage frequency.
* Steps for successful onboarding include:
    1. Define goals and milestonesSimplify the customer journey
    2. Get to initial value quickly
    3. Help prospects with empty state during initial signup
    4. Define PQLs
    5. Personalize onboarding with custom journeys
    6. Nurture with personalized engagement, such as behavior-based communication, time-based triggers, and e-mails or in-product messaging
    7. Document important customer journeys

8. Measure and track prospects through onboarding—where they fall off, and at what rates they complete onboarding
- Shorten the time it takes prospects to reach the PQL stage by:
  - Prioritizing in-product behaviors based on their value to you and your customers
  - Automating self-service checkout
  - Initiating just-in-time personalized engagements
  - Prioritizing target accounts with a higher potential to close
  - Delivering thought leadership at every stage of the customer lifecycle
  - Using targeted product demos

Chapter 10
Product-Led Customer Retention and Expansion

The customer lifecycle is a continuous process, and it's challenging to rigidly define where the acquisition, adoption, retention, and expansion stages begin and end. Often, we associate customer retention with the renewal event—when a customer renews their subscription. But the process of retention, as well as adoption and expansion, starts when prospects and customers experience your product from initial signup. Prospects and customers make judgments based on, for example, how they experience your free trial and onboarding process.

Customer success departments are typically accountable for retention and expansion, but this is changing with the SaaS evolution. With a product-led approach, customer success accountability spans the entire customer lifecycle and is supported by cross-functional teams, including product, marketing, sales, and service.

The first step to product-led customer success is to know your product champion. A product champion is often the person who signs up for a trial and involves appropriate buying personas in the process. Ensure that you share the complete customer onboarding plan with this person because he or she will be instrumental in its implementation and organization-wide adoption.

Since the product champion usually has the highest level of engagement with your product, this person's success with your product is essential. Because this champion is backing your product, he feels responsible for making sure it satisfies his organization's needs, and he will be more likely to continue promoting use of your product if he can use it to do his job better or more effectively.

If the product champion is not a daily end user, your company should find the most active and engaged user that fits the role of the champion. We believe that product champions are very active users with a demonstrated level of expertise with your product. These people often transition to "advocates" later in their customer lifecycle.

Applying a product-led approach will help you predict which product champion (and their organizations) is more likely to renew, as well as who will likely churn based on declining engagement and usage.

10.1 How to Improve Customer Retention and Expansion

In carrying on with our theme of providing you with practical, tactical recommendations, here is what you can do to improve the results of your retention and expansion efforts.

1. Orchestrate customer onboarding

As mentioned earlier, customer (or organization) onboarding is slightly different from prospect onboarding. The primary goal of onboarding prospects is to educate them on your product and the value it provides. You should remove anything that interferes with realizing initial value.

Customer onboarding requires a close evaluation of how the whole account (i.e., organization) can create and experience value by using your product. At the same time, you may need a separate customer onboarding process that gets select individuals within an account up and running. The ultimate goal here would be to create customer advocates that help you promote your product within the broader organization. Here are a couple of questions to keep in mind to help you determine which customer onboarding process(es) you need to design:

> How many people in your customer's organization will benefit from using your product?
>
> Is your product valuable for cross-functional teams?

Ensure that the appropriate people are invited
Create a list of users within each account that could benefit from having access to your product, and understand their personas. One way to create the list is by talking to the product champion in each account. More often than not, this person has a good understanding of who will be using your product in the organization, as well as the roles of each user. Another option is to come up with the list through your product experience—for instance, when you send automated e-mails to users, you can ask if anyone else within the recipient's organization needs to get involved in the task they are working on. With a complete list of prospective users in your customer's organization, you can understand what is needed to encourage adoption of your product, as well as how to expand usage.

Consider how your product can engage prospects as they are completing a specific product task with messages that ask if anyone on their team needs to approve the next step. Basically, you need to find a way to involve key people as part of a specific flow where their input might be required.

Here's how it might look. Let's use Expensify as an example. Its software helps with expense management. In this case, the main user is an accounts receivables professional. Perhaps as this person is working on a step in the expense management process, your product shows a message suggesting that the CFO needs to approve the task. If the CFO isn't yet using your product, your product could automatically send an invite with the assigned action.

> TIP: Make a target list of all people in your customer's organization that should be using your product. If they aren't using it now, create a plan to engage them. You may help a larger portion of the customer's organization learn about, use, and come to depend on your product.

Review assigned admin and user roles

If your product is going to handle the sensitive process of direct communication with your prospects and customers, you need to clearly define roles and permissions. This will help prevent your teams from making errors and communication missteps. Here's an example of what these roles and permissions might look like:

1. Editor: Can create content and prepare engagements (e.g., e-mails, messages, etc.) for approval
2. Reviewer: Can view content engagements for accuracy and relevance in regard to target audiences
3. Approver: Can view content and engagements and approve use
4. Executor: Can launch the engagement

Depending on the size of your organization, you could assign these permissions and roles to one or multiple people. It is typical to see these split into two primary roles of Content Editor/Reviewer and Approver/Executor.

Integrate with customer's data systems and third-party resources

Most products can provide more value when they're integrated with the customer's data and workflow systems. When that is the case, it's important to ensure that the customer implements all necessary integrations.

> TIP: Create a list of critical integrations, and design a process to ensure customers complete this process.

Train every user in your customer's organization

The more customers use your product, the more dependent and engaged they will become. Training can play a critical role in getting your customers to use your product regularly. With a product-led approach, cross-functional teams can monitor customer segments and their interactions, and use available data to educate customers with guides and messaging as they use the product. From an internal development and training perspective, your customer support team can be more effective by digging into the journey of a specific user to understand, for example, what might have gone wrong if the customer's usage drops off.

Customer onboarding checklist:

☐ Invite teammates and set up admin and access preferences
☐ Integrate with customer's systems and third-party data sources
☐ Train everyone in your customer's organization
☐ Ask your customer to share their goals and objectives, so your team can track success
☐ Set payment process

NOTE: While we are not covering the last two steps, they are critical parts of the onboarding process.

2. Closely monitor user behavior

In part 3, we described the idea of a Value Gap, which is a discrepancy between what a customer expects and what is actually received (or their perception of what they received). In most cases, a Value Gap is a result of a decline in customer engagement in general because this often prevents them from experiencing your product's most important features.

In order to ensure that customers gain value while using your product, your company must pay attention to how frequently customers use your product and which features they turn to the most.

To get at this understanding, answer the following:

· How often do your most profitable customers log in?
· What features and product-usage frequencies correlate with renewals?
· What early customer behavior signs can inform an upsell and cross-sell strategy?
· What usage metrics help predict a user's desire to upgrade their current subscription?

Understanding user behaviors enables your teams to anticipate issues that may cause customers to taper off (or increase) their usage of your product. It also empowers them to design behavior-based triggers that automatically activate in-product messages or e-mails that encourage engagement at the appropriate moments.

Here are examples of scenarios your teams can monitor and design behavior-based triggers around:

- Decline in engagement
- Increase in engagement
- Reaching usage limit
- Readiness to upgrade

TIP: Create competency around understanding your product's valued features, engagement frequencies, and other customer behavior data that correlate with higher CLV via renewals, upsells, and cross-sells.

3. Focus on continuous product adoption and customer nurturing

Product adoption and customer nurturing are continuous processes. As product teams release new features and capabilities, your current customers should be learning about and adopting them right away.

A product-led approach allows your product teams to deliver valuable features to the market sooner, and that matters, because the longer you wait to ship, the less value is received by your customers. The product-led approach enables this, because your product team is continuously getting feedback from customers and prospects actually using the product—even immediately after new product updates and releases.

A critical aspect of this is ensuring timely engagement with prospects and customers about new product releases. For example, rather than wait three days to inform customers about a valuable new feature, it's best to inform them right away within the product, so they will have context for better understanding on how to take advantage of it.

Summing up, product adoption and customer nurturing work best when you continually engage customers throughout the lifecycle and deliver relevant, contextual messages in a timely manner.

4. Anticipate renewal, upgrade, and cross-sell opportunities with behavior-based analytics

Behavior-based analytics provide companies with a better way to predict the right time to ask a customer for a renewal or upgrade.

Traditionally, the customer success team is responsible for managing retention and expansion of existing customers by periodically contacting each account. However, this approach is time-consuming and ineffective, and it doesn't scale well. A better way is to monitor customers for specific product behaviors that correlate with higher renewal and upgrade rates. Once these behaviors occur, you call upon automated, trigger-based engagement, either within the product or outside of the product via an established digital channel such as e-mail.

For example, if your pricing tiers are based on certain usage, then reaching the upper threshold of usage can be an effective trigger to automate an in-product or e-mail message prompting the customer to upgrade.

Many companies are already using some product analytics to initiate contact at the right moment with a customer. However, it's time-consuming to gather product analytics and then build campaigns to act on this data—and timing is critical. The cost of delay between the time when a company analyzes the data and then creates a response can be a major factor in how successful efforts are to grow customers.

A product-led strategy enables teams to shorten the time between customer action and appropriate response using built-in, automated, and scalable means. Plus, it allows them to improve how the response is delivered. In-product notifications are far more effective than e-mail in getting the customer's attention, because the message is more contextual.

Retaining and growing customers in the SaaS industry is the most important factor for driving CLV. A product-led strategy not only enables companies to monitor customer behaviors that correlate with retaining and growing customers, but it also helps them minimize the time it takes to deliver the right message to the right customer segment at the right time.

5. Apply break-even analysis

Using break even analysis helps teams understand how quickly a customer becomes profitable— and the time in which CLV exceeds the CAC. A product-led approach enables companies to track the customer journey and correlate behavior data with shorter time to breakeven point.

Product-led GTM is a continuous process

With a product-led GTM, customer acquisition is a continuous process that provides valuable feedback on what to build next, how to design strategic messages, what price to charge, and how to drive customers through their lifecycles in more profitable and efficient ways.

In Figure 8.1, we summarize all the steps companies must address across all stages of the customer lifecycle (we covered this previously, in Chapter 4). As an organization calls upon a product-led strategy to learn about and optimize the customer acquisition process, it can use the feedback and findings to adjust other GTM elements. These can include target customer, messaging, product offering, and pricing. In other words, a product-led strategy is a practical way for organizations to receive feedback that they can use to further optimize all aspects of a scalable and repeatable GTM strategy.

10.2 Key Takeaways

- Retention, adoption and expansion all start when customers experience your product from initial signup.
- Identify your product champions and share the entire customer onboarding experience with them.
- To improve customer retention and expansion with a product-led GTM strategy:
  - Orchestrate customer onboarding—educate customers on the product and its value
  - Invite the people who will most benefit from using your product
  - Review assigned and user roles
  - Integrate with the customer's data system and third-party data sources
  - Train every user in the customer's organization
- Closely monitor user behavior for frequency and use of specific features.
- Continually engage customers throughout the lifecycle and deliver relevant, contextual messages in a timely manner.
- Anticipate renewal, upgrade, and cross-sell opportunities by monitoring customer behavior and connecting via digital channels such as e-mail.
- Apply break-even analysis to discover how quickly a customer becomes profitable.

Chapter 11
The Anatomy of Personalized Customer Engagement

A product-led GTM strategy is all about optimizing the customer acquisition process through personalized customer experiences and engagements. Designing those personalized customer experiences the right way is key to scaling and making the customer acquisition process more repeatable.

You can achieve this goal by combining customer segmentation, customer journeys, and nurturing.

11.1 Customer Segmentation

The two primary aspects of customer segmentation are demographics and behavioral data.

Segmentation = Demographics + Behavioral Data

This is not a new idea. However, when we talk about a product-led approach to customer acquisition, we emphasize the importance of in-product behavior. This is in contrast to behavior that happens in cross-channel marketing environments, including interactions with ads, e-mail opens, website visits, and so forth.

In-product customer behavior unlocks insights into the needs and values of your prospects and customers. (For a step-by-step process on segmenting customers, see this detailed article— "CUSTOMER SEGMENTATION: A GUIDE TO THE BEST B2B PRACTICES"[1]). A product-led strategy enhances the effectiveness of traditional segmentation. In addition, it enables you to better track and measure the performance of a particular segment throughout the customer lifecycle, including revenue impact and CLV vs. CAC ratio.

11.2 Customer Journey and Velocity

It's critical for companies to map in-product customer journeys, because they can uncover important customer segments and needs based on the sequence of events and actions taken by customers on their way to achieving a goal.

For example, say your company provides a solution to streamline expense reports. Your teams originally designed a "first expense report" customer journey that required users to navigate four pages and five clicks. However, a large portion of your users reach this desired outcome in eight clicks. Seeing this, you could segment these users, and closely guide them through this process with a tutorial or walkthroughs. This use case illustrates an effective way to collaborate and experiment within the product before designing completely new product experiences.

Behavioral data also includes production data and customer journeys. Knowing that prospects interacted with a product feature is helpful. Connecting these insights with customer subscription data enables your teams to be more intelligent.

Most product analytics solutions tell you how a certain user or segment interacts with a product or feature. However, you must also know their subscription level, or how much revenue comes from the segment of customers that experience difficulties using the product—for example, if they need to take extra (i.e., too many) steps to execute a core action, such as sending an expense report. Without connecting these different data points, it is hard to estimate potential churn and revenue impact.

Mapping customer journeys helps teams understand whether product flows and features make sense to customers. The speed at which prospects move through the core journey enables your company to make some assumptions about the level of pain they are experiencing, as well as their buying intent.

> TIP: Map customer journeys that lead to important desired outcomes; understand how quickly customers travel through these journeys and any associated risk of losing customers before they reach their goals.

11.3 In-Product Behavior and Habit Creation

In-product behavior is essential to personalized customer experiences, as it is the first step for influencing prospect and customer habit. Dr. BJ Fogg, the creator of "**THE FOGG BEHAVIORAL MODEL**"[2], outlined three elements that must occur for behaviors to change: motivation, ability, and trigger. Your users need all three before your product will become an essential part of their daily lives.

Although you normally want more product usage, there are some cases when the less customers use the product, the more value they receive. For example, a product that sends an automated notification to customers when something is broken can be seen as valuable when the customers receive fewer of these notifications. However, for most software products, the more customers are engaged inside a product, the more value they experience.

With a product-led strategy, we filter out less-motivated prospects by asking them to sign up for a product. Assuming motivation is there, do prospects have the ability to execute actions leading to initial value? And when they realize initial value (which is the desired outcome), what triggers can be used to encourage a prospect or customer to repeat this action so they experience follow-on value?

Let's take Salesforce as an example. Marc Benioff has done a tremendous job making the Salesforce brand the most synonymous with CRM. Every organization needs CRM—it's where organizations aggregate customer relationship data. When a company starts reaching out to customers, the obvious question arises: Where do we keep track of all customer data and interactions? This is one of a few triggers that Salesforce uses effectively to create desire and a habit for their CRM solution.

To understand how triggers can help your company re-engage prospects and customers with your product, document a day in the life of your target customer. For example, at Aptrinsic, our goal is to connect with product leaders that make daily decisions about product features and messaging. We use this decision process as a trigger to encourage them to use our platform.

Ideally, a product team will turn to Aptrinsic when it is seeking ways to improve the onboarding experience, and product managers will log into Aptrinsic as they are planning which features to update. Within Aptrinsic, they can determine which features are used most often by customers, and how much revenue is associated with these features, to make the optimal decision. In other words, we want our customers to turn to Aptrinsic automatically whenever they are trying to improve their own products—just as so many of us automatically turn to Amazon when we want to buy a book online, or how so many businesspeople now turn to Slack if they need to collaborate with co-workers. Ultimately, every SaaS company should be focused on making their users turn to their products automatically and habitually. In other words, make users want to return to the product over and over again.

> TIP: Describe a day in the life of your ideal customer to understand how your product fits in, and what triggers will cause the customer to re-engage with your product.

11.4 Moment of Joy

The gaming industry provides great examples of companies succeeding with product-led GTM strategies. The most successful gaming companies offer a free version of their game. They then engage, delight, and convert users through a variety of strategies, such as selling in-game goods, advancing paid users, or unlocking certain features. These are all triggers for realizing a Moment of Joy, which is the same as the Moment of Truth we spoke about earlier—the time when a prospect feels the value in the product.

Consider this: "Experienced gaming analysts know[3], for instance, that players who complete a number of actions during the same session have a significantly higher likelihood for a FTD [first-time deposit] as well as a higher retention rate." In other words, that Moment of Truth is when companies are in the best position to convert a prospect into a paying customer.

One key to a successful, product-led conversion is to cultivate moments of joy with recognition and rewards when a user performs a desired action. We are not advocating that you use gamification as part of your SaaS product. However, it's worth noting that game producers are driving success by being ultra-focused on getting players into the game early and incentivizing them in creative ways to pay. SaaS companies can learn how to better engage prospects in their products by understanding how gaming companies approach monetization[4].

SaaS companies should keep in mind that core actions and product features can bring valuable rewards to customers and prospects if delivered in the right context at the right time. Users can genuinely feel better about themselves, their work, and your product. Some companies celebrate such achievements with in-product congratulations messages, and by highlighting milestones as they are achieved.

In its analysis of how software companies scale quickly[5], OpenView Investments discovered three ways Slack is smart about the in-product experience:

- During the onboarding process, new users are taken through a tutorial when they first log in.
- The Help Center lays out next steps for new customers.
- Triggered in-app messaging encourages freemium users to convert to paid customers once they've reached their usage limit.

You could have purchased 119,982 pounds of bananas with your salary this year. Did you know that bananas are potassium superfruits? One banana contains 13% of the daily suggested amount of potassium.

Even incorporating small things into your product can make the experience more personal for users. Let's look at Gusto, a human resources management solution. Users can see and experience cool personalized messages that make it fun to use Gusto. For example, in the sidebar, Gusto calculates how many pounds of bananas you can buy with your salary—a nice way to entertain customers.

Slack does a great job incorporating messages that make it more joyful to use its product. The Slack signup process ends with this feel-good message:

Slack's loading screen has a personality too:

Loading ..
Sometimes you eat the bear and sometimes the bear, well, he eats you.

Welcome, Myk Pono

You just created **Aptrinsic** on Slack. Next, we'll show you how to get the conversation going – it only takes a minute or two!

Let's go

Bottom line: When a prospect or customer reaches the desired outcome, use this opportunity to celebrate with them by creating small moments of joy. These intrinsic rewards will make your customers feel more empowered and improve their perception of your product's value.

TIP: Identify core use cases and journeys where your team can create joyful moments to reinforce the value delivered with the product.

11.5 Nurturing and Contextual Engagements

In a traditional GTM strategy, the customer acquisition process relies heavily on nurturing leads via activities outside of the product, and is not typically supported by behavioral data within the product. With a product-led GTM strategy, your nurturing is driven by real-time contextual insights.

Nurturing (or drip e-mail) campaigns within a product-led GTM strategy are triggered by the customer's in-product action or inaction. Contextual engagement happens when the right customer receives the right messages at the right time through the right channel.

Figure 11.1 - The Structure of Contextual Engagement

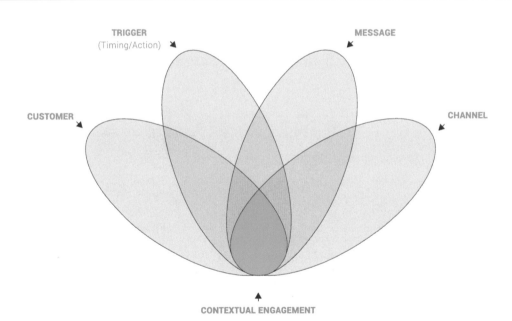

Let's analyze what we mean by contextual engagement with the example depicted in Figure 11.1:

CUSTOMER (WHO): Someone at his tenth day in a free trial process

TRIGGER (WHEN): Hasn't completed the journey to initial value

MESSAGE (WHAT): Show the benefits of reaching initial value

CHANNEL (WHERE): In-product message + e-mail for a personalized experience

A customer reaches the tenth day of a free trial and hasn't yet completed the journey to initial value. This triggers an in-product message and/or e-mail describing and illustrating the benefits of completing the journey. For inspiration, here's an example[6] of one of these e-mails from a company called RunKeeper offering a fitness app. The e-mail starts by pointing out that the recipient hasn't used the app recently, and includes tips to get started.

11.6 The Importance of Omnichannel and Real-Time Personalization

You're probably familiar with a multi-channel approach to customer acquisition, including social media, PR, website, and events; but a multi-channel approach doesn't necessarily mean the customer experience, when it comes to messages and CTAs, is consistent from one channel to another. That's because these channels are often managed in a siloed fashion. On the other hand, an omnichannel approach is designed to enable consistent experiences across all channels and devices.

An omnichannel approach helps companies create contextual engagement that looks and feels the same for customers across channels and devices. For example, an engagement with a specific customer segment can be simultaneously delivered via in-product messages, e-mails, and a mobile application; and with an omnichannel experience, you can easily know if a customer or prospect is on your website, logged into your product, or not engaging with you, so you can decide which channel to use.

The time that it takes for a company to create personalized engagement as a response to a prospect's in-product behavior is a critical factor in the success of this engagement. If it takes a couple of days to pull relevant data and create an engagement response, the prospect might have already moved on. Acting in real time is critical in these situations.

Companies that find a way to create automated personalized engagement based on customer segments and behavior will more quickly get feedback and gather valuable analytics.

11.7 Experimentation and Optimization

The idea of experimentation isn't new for marketers. However, with a product-led GTM strategy, companies can design experiments that test not only ads and landing pages, but also the whole experience, including onboarding and free trial requirements. For example, Salesforce can create a personalized onboarding process for an small-and-medium business (SMB) company versus a large enterprise.

Stephen Pavlovich, CEO of Conversion.com, explains how experimentation enables companies to gather valuable data that they can't get anywhere else. He also outlines how it can help drive product growth[7].

11.8 Key Takeaways

There are eight ways to personalize customer engagement:

1. **Segmentation: Based on demographic and behavioral data, including interaction with ads, e-mail opens, and website visits.**
2. **Customer Journey and Velocity: Understand how quickly customers travel through product journeys, and personalize these journeys to help them reach their goals.**
3. **In-product Behavior and Habits: Understand the how three essential elements— motivation, ability, and trigger—apply to your customer's day.**
4. **Moment of Joy: Create joyful moments and use personalized messages to make customers feel empowered.**
5. **Nurturing and Contextual Engagements: Based on in-product action, know the who, when, what, and where to help customers complete their journeys.**
6. **Omnichannel and Real-time: Create and quickly deliver contextual engagements that look consistent across channels.**
7. **Personalize Everything: Every aspect of a GTM strategy and the marketing mix can be personalized.**
8. **Experimentation: Experiment to gather valuable data that you can't get anywhere else.**

Chapter 12

The Anatomy of a Product-Led Organization

A product-led GTM strategy requires a complete alignment of product, marketing, sales, and success teams in an organization. Key to this approach is being hyper-focused on delivering personalized customer experiences based on in-product behavior and usage patterns.

Just as it was marketing automation's mission to better align sales and marketing as we moved from a sales-led to a marketing-led strategy, it will be the job of product experience platforms to align sales, marketing, customer success, and now, product. This creates the triad needed to really improve customer experience and efficiency.

Note: To be successful with a product-led GTM strategy, it must become part of your organizational DNA. A leadership team should lead this change in your company, providing all necessary guidance and resources to align all key departments. If the CEO can't ensure this alignment, is there another C-level role tasked with solving this?

Let's consider how teams have to adjust their playbooks to succeed with a product-led GTM strategy.

12.1 Product Playbook

Because product teams are part of the customer acquisition process with a product-led approach, they can make key decisions about what product features to build next based on in-depth customer behavior taken from the product.

SaaS companies release updates and new features on a weekly, daily, and in some extreme cases, hourly basis; but a product team's success is no longer measured by simply delivering features on time and on budget. Today, product success can be measured based on product adoption and customer engagement metrics. This is why the role of product leaders is changing, and they are viewed more as the mini-CEOs of the product, as McKinsey & Company pointed out in the article **"PRODUCT MANAGERS FOR THE DIGITAL WORLD"**[1].

Some product teams will need to make a huge mental shift to execute on a product-led strategy. SaaS companies who sell into sales and marketing organizations have always understood the need to support growth from a product perspective, but it's not nearly as obvious to some product teams, who mostly think about selling to personas. More product teams need to think about making customer growth a much larger priority in the roadmaps. A product-led approach can help them do that, guiding them to understand which personas actually use the company's product and the profitability of these personas.

Making informed decisions about what to build next

By maintaining a unified customer profile with detailed in-product behavior, product teams can better understand their customers, what features they actually use, and how often they use them. Customer journeys provide insights into how users navigate through your product and what new features or updates will encourage higher adoption. By leveraging capabilities such as a feature heatmap, product teams can identify the most valuable features that directly impact revenue. This allows the product organization to align its development efforts to increase sales and market acceptance. A product-led GTM strategy enables product teams to create what Jeff Gothelf and Josh Seiden referred to in their book **SENSE AND RESPOND**[2] as outcome-based roadmaps. In a nutshell, these are focused on driving product engagement metrics, rather than delivering certain features.

Guiding customers to use your product

You can improve product adoption by using customer segmentation based on behavioral and product usage data. This enables your product teams to create more personalized onboarding experiences, foster initial value with various cohorts, and get new features adopted more quickly.

Collecting relevant feedback from the right customers

With a product-led approach, the product itself becomes a primary method of engaging and interacting with customers. In-product engagements are highly contextual, and create a nearly real-time feedback loop between companies and their prospects and customers. This two-way communication process makes product teams more agile and enables product experimentation by releasing new features for specific segments.

Product teams can then determine the effectiveness of their strategies by reviewing in-product surveys, triggered feedback, and the Customer Behavior Index (CBI). (CBI is a metric that helps you determine how engaged your prospects and customers are based on their in-product activity and usage. More on this in Chapter 13.) Together, these provide a clear understanding of customer satisfaction and the overall health of the account.

Assigning product operational responsibility

In most SaaS companies, marketing operations and sales operations teams are responsible for setting up technologies and processes so the larger marketing and sales teams can handle everyday tasks more efficiently.

We believe that a shift to product-led strategies may lead to the creation of a product operations role. This role will be responsible for supporting the product, marketing, and sales teams by setting up processes, workflows, and technologies to streamline user segmentation, engagement campaigns, and product experimentation. It's conceivable that some of the existing operational roles in the organization will be repurposed to better align marketing, sales, customer success, and product teams' responsibilities. This will help ensure that all departments have access to the same unified customer data to create consistent omnichannel experiences for customers.

12.2 Marketing Playbook

We believe that, as a new organizational culture emerges geared toward generating PQLs, this new customer-centric approach will fuel the next evolution of GTM strategies. This will move marketing away from mass lead demand generation, to tactics focused on creating and curating customer experiences. This approach is more efficient and more CAC-effective, and increases CLV for companies.

Focusing on product signups

Knowing which customer segments are the most engaged helps marketing teams build campaigns that better target customers to increase retention, thus increasing CLV potential. With a product-led strategy, marketing teams can also build better retargeting campaigns, focusing on the most valuable accounts.

Focusing on the right segments and nurturing prospects to PQLs

Vanity metrics, such as website visits and scoring leads based on whether a prospect opens an e-mail, do not provide marketers with an accurate picture of the most profitable target customers. Instead, a product-led strategy enables marketing teams to understand prospects on the behavioral level, and build strategies to attract the most profitable segments. Marketing teams that build automated behavior-based triggers during the nurturing phase can better engage potential customers. Automation reduces the response time between user behavior and an appropriate engagement campaign, and generating demand from the right customer segments can in turn drive more efficient and better marketing ROI.

Developing thought leadership content based on customer in-product behavior
Insight into prospect and customer behaviors and feedback helps marketing create more effective thought leadership content. Additionally, they can use in-product communication as another channel for engaging potential and existing customers with relevant and helpful content.

12.3 Sales playbook

The highest value a sales team can receive with the product-led approach is to know when it is the right time for prospects and customers to buy, renew, and/or upgrade, based on in-product behavior. The role of the sales organization may shift toward a more consultative approach to selling, where SDRs and AEs will focus on helping prospects get started, and educating them on product and best practices.

Prioritize PQLs and improve forecast
In-product behavior provides a more accurate signal of buying intent, which helps sales better prioritize opportunities. At the same time, sales teams that determine the stage of each prospect on their trial and adoption journeys can improve forecast accuracy.

Optimize the land-and-expand strategy
With a product-led strategy, sales teams are better equipped to drive low-touch prospects to self-service and focus resources on the expansion of highly valuable accounts.

2.4 Customer Success Playbook

Customer success teams face the difficult challenge of piecing together customer data and building workflows for manual outreach to customers. The product-led approach helps these teams more proactively battle churn rates by taking advantage of automated in-product triggers based on relevant in-product behaviors.

Improve customer onboarding and training
Customer onboarding and training can be improved with a better understanding of individual users and the account as a whole. Even when a personal training session is required, customer behavioral data allows customer success teams to be more prepared. For example, the customer

success team can monitor where customers fall off the journey to achieving a core goal (such as creating and sending an expense report), and proactively help by guiding the customer in-product. Similarly, if the customer success team has an upcoming call with a customer, it can review her in-product behaviors to identify potential issues. The team can then help her resolve those during their discussion.

Prevent customer support issues

As mentioned above, customer success teams can closely track how customers use the product and where they experience difficulty. Doing so, and then proactively addressing these issues, can reduce the number of support tickets and requests. Consider the case of RapidMiner, which offers a SaaS app for data science teams. The company tracks user error rates and notifies its Customer Success Manager (CSR) if a customer exceeds a predefined threshold of errors within a single hour. The CSR then proactively reaches out to the customer. By helping customers understand how to avoid errors, and instead, best use RapidMiner to achieve their goals, the company minimizes both support requests and churn rates associated with user frustration.

12.5 Key Takeaways

- A product-led GTM strategy requires a complete alignment of the product, marketing, sales, and customer success teams, along with changes to the team playbooks.
- The product playbook will use a unified customer profile based on detailed in-product behavior to decide what to build next, and learn how new features and updates are adopted. A new product operations role could evolve—one that supports all of the teams with processes, workflows, and technologies.
- The marketing playbook will focus on product signups, nurturing prospects to PQLs, and developing thought leadership content based on in-product behavior.
- The sales playbook will learn from in-product behavior when customers are ready to buy, renew, and/or upgrade, which will allow sales to then prioritize PQLs and optimize their land-and-expand strategies.
- The customer success playbook lays out how to piece together customer data and build workflows for manual customer outreach. This team will need to improve customer onboarding and training, while working to prevent customer support issues.

Chapter 13
Metrics: Measuring Success with a Product-Led GTM

Peter Drucker, one of the most famous management consultants of the last century, once said: "You can't manage what you can't measure."

There is plenty of material available on SaaS metrics; we will reference a few valuable resources in this section. However, it's important to keep in mind that a product-led GTM strategy, as we have shown throughout this book, changes the traditional sales funnel, replacing MQLs and SQLs with PQLs. Moreover, a product-led approach enables teams to track and measure in-product customer behaviors and correlate them with crucial SaaS metrics, such as CLV, CAC, and others.

Simply put, a product-led approach slightly changes the focus of what and how we measure success and effectiveness. SaaS companies are unique in how they acquire and retain customers. They invest significant resources in acquiring customers up front, and then recover the costs and realize revenue through the lifetime relationship with each customer. First, let's look closely at how to track customer progression through a lifecycle.

13.1 Step 1: Tracking Customer Progression Through a Lifecycle

A product-led strategy changes how companies track the effectiveness of customers moving through different lifecycle stages: from signup to PQL, from PQL to customer, and from customer to active customer. Each ratio helps identify bottlenecks in the lifecycle where customers experience a value gap and fall off the process.

With a product-led customer acquisition strategy, companies start gathering valuable behavior data early in the customer lifecycle, which increases team effectiveness in re-engaging customers with the product. By understanding conversion processes along the customer lifecycle, companies can design timely engagement campaigns to encourage customers to return to, and actively use, their product.

Let's quickly review the seven user states in the customer lifecycle:

Table 13.1 - Customer States in a Lifecycle

1. Visitor	A visitor is anyone who lands on your website.
2. Signup/Trial (prospect)	A prospect is any visitor who signs up for a free trial or freemium offering.
3. PQL (activated user/prospect)	An engaged prospect reaches PQL state and signals readiness to become a customer.
4. Customer	A customer is someone who purchases your product.
5. Active Customer	An active customer is a customer with a high Customer Behavior Index (CBI) that correlates with a high probability of renewal and/or upgrading.
6. Renewed/Retained	A customer that renewed, upgraded, or expanded the product subscription.
7. Churned	A customer that stopped subscribing or canceled a subscription service.

The initial goal for SaaS companies is to convert visitors to signups. At signup stage, the team can collect profile, company, and in-product behavioral data. Using this data allows teams to deliver timely engagements with the customer through in-product, mobile, or e-mail messages. Then companies can nurture prospects until they show enough interest in the product based on their product usage. Prospects that reach PQL stage are engaged by the sales team to assist in buying or in helping them increase product usage. Tracking customer behavior inside the product enables companies to predict and mitigate customer churn, and forecast CLV.

But let's take a step back and explore how tracking conversion rates is an effective way to understand how prospects and customers progress through the customer lifecycle.

Measuring Effectiveness with Conversion Rates
Conversion rate from one state to the next in the lifecycle helps companies understand what part of the lifecycle can be improved. At the same time, sales can more accurately forecast when they understand conversion rates.

Let's review the basic conversion rates that companies have to track to understand how successful they are in progressing a prospect through the customer lifecycle.

Visitor-to-Signup Rate is the percentage of visitors that visit your page and then sign up. It is calculated by dividing the number of product signups by the number of visitors to a signup page. The visitor-to-signup rate shows how effectively your company convinces visitors to sign up for free trials or a freemium.

Signup-to-PQL Rate is the percentage of prospects that complete profile and in-product engagement requirements to become PQLs. It is calculated by dividing the number of PQLs by the number of signups. The signup-to-PQL rate provides insights into how effectively your company engages prospects in the early stages of reaching initial value.

NOTE: In some cases, it makes sense to analyze signup-to-PQL rate in terms of individual and account signups.

PQL-to-Customer Rate is the percentage of PQLs that convert to customers. It is calculated by dividing the number of customers by the number of PQLs. The PQL-to-customer rate shows how effectively your company converts PQLs to customers.

Signup-to-Customer Rate is the percentage of signups that become paying customers. It is calculated by dividing the number of customers by the number of signups. The signup-to-customer rate shows how your company, on average, converts signups to customers.

Customer Churn Rate is the percentage of customers lost due to churn (i.e., cancellation or failure to renew). It is calculated by dividing the number of churned customers by the number of customers at the start of the period for which the churn rate is calculated.

Monthly Recurring Revenue (MRR) Churn Rate (a.k.a. Gross Revenue Churn) is the percentage of MRR revenue lost from existing customers at the start of the period for which MRR churn is calculated. MRR churn rate is always positive (positive churn rate means the company loses money), because it does not include upsell and cross-sell.

MRR Expansion Rate (aka Net Revenue Retention Rate) is the percentage of MRR that is gained due to upsells and cross-sells to existing customers for the period for which MRR expansion is calculated. It is calculated by dividing the amount of expansion MRR by the starting MRR.

Net MRR Churn (a.k.a. Net Revenue Churn) is the percentage of MRR change based on churned and expansion MRR for the same period. It is calculated by subtracting expansion MRR from churned MRR and dividing that by MRR at the start of the period. Net MRR churn is the percentage of MRR lost from existing customers in a period.

When measuring churn, we need to remember that positive churn means that the company is losing customers and revenue, and negative churn means the opposite—the company generates more revenue from upsell and cross-sell than it loses to churn.

The table below summarizes these conversion and effectiveness metrics.

Table 13.2 - Effectiveness Metrics

Visitor-to-Signup Rate	Visitor-to-signup rate = # of signups/# of visitors on the signup page
Signup-to-PQL Rate	Signup-to-PQL rate = # of PQLs/# of signups
PQL-to-Customer Rate	PQL-to-customer rate = # of customers/# of PQLs
Signup-to-Customer Rate	Signup-to-customer rate = # of customers/# of signups
Customer Churn Rate	Customer churn rate = # of churned customers/total # of customers at the start of the period
MRR Churn Rate	MRR churn rate = churned MRR/starting MRR
MRR Expansion Rate	MRR expansion rate = expansion MRR/starting MRR
Net MRR Churn Rate	Net MRR churn rate = (churned MRR - expansion MRR)/starting MRR

Differentiating between customer and revenue churn rates is important. It is possible for a company to experience both a positive customer churn rate (i.e., the company lost customers) and a negative net MRR churn rate (i.e., the company generated more revenues from new customers than the revenues it lost from churned customers). This situation can be caused by the company deliberately moving up-market, selling to larger companies at a higher average selling price while losing smaller and less profitable customers. Another common cause for achieving both a positive customer churn rate and negative net MRR churn rate is a rise in prices that drives smaller customers to churn, but extracts more revenue from larger accounts.

As Tom Tunguz, partner at Redpoint, explains, negative churn can be a powerful growth mechanism[1].

Breaking down churn metrics

Churn and retention metrics can be calculated in multiple ways; we have provided the most common measurements. While many in the SaaS industry are aware of the importance of tracking churn rate, let's highlight a few reasons why.

A high churn rate can drive a SaaS company out of business. Acquiring a new customer is always more expensive than retaining an existing one. For SaaS businesses, keeping existing customers is even more critical, because if a customer leaves before the break-even point, the company loses money. The longer a customer stays with the company, the higher revenue margins the company realizes.

In the traditional GTM model, the customer success team is in charge of managing churn. Often, customer success teams use Net Promoter Scores (NPS) and product analytics to plan how to follow up with customers. The problem with this approach is that customer success solutions only show forensics data on customer behavior, piecing the data puzzle together after the fact. On the other hand, a product-led customer acquisition process allows teams to monitor customer engagement as it occurs and proactively deliver engagements that reduce the probability of churn.

Let's look at a simple example of how a fictional SaaS company calculates its churn rate.

Table 13.3 - Churn Rate Example

Total # of customers at the start of the period	1000	**Starting MRR**	**$200,000**	Customer Churn Rate	4.00%
# of churned customers	-40	Churned MRR	-$25,000	MRR Churn	12.50%
# of new customers	100	New MRR	$20,000	MRR Expansion	22.50%
Net new customers	60	Expansion MRR	$45,000	Net MRR Churn	-10.00%
Total # of customers at the end of the period	1060	Net New MRR	$40,000		
		Ending MRR	**$240,000**		

You can find a more detailed analysis of churn metrics in the iconic post "**SAAS METRICS 2.0 – A GUIDE TO MEASURING AND IMPROVING WHAT MATTERS**"[2] by David Skok, general partner with Matrix Partners.

Measuring the velocity of customer lifecycle
VELOCITY METRICS describe how long it takes a company to achieve certain milestones. This includes the average number of days it takes a prospect to go from signup to becoming a PQL, and the average number of months it takes a company to break even (when CLV>CAC).

Understanding how long it takes for prospects and customers to move from one customer lifecycle state to another helps companies in two ways. They can better forecast revenue and also understand what part of the lifecycle is the longest and how to shorten it.

Customer lifecycle length is the average number of days that takes a prospect or customer to advance to the next stage. Let's review a few critical metrics within this lifecycle:

Days from signup to PQL measures the average number of days it takes a prospect to become a PQL.

Days from PQL to customer measures the average number of days it takes a PQL to become a customer.

Days from signup to customer measures the average number of days it takes a prospect to become a customer.

Days to break-even measures the average number of days it takes a customer to generate enough revenue to cover the CAC. In other words, it shows how quickly a company recovers its CAC.

Average customer life is the total time (in days) of a relationship between a customer and a company. It measures the average number of days (or months) between the day a prospect becomes a customer and when that customer churns (or cancels).

The table below provides examples of customer acquisition metrics.

Table 13.4 - Customer Acquisition Funnel Metrics

		Conversion rate		Customer lifecycle length	
Visitors	10,000				
Signups	750	7.5%	visitor-to-signup		
PQLs	150	20.0%	signup-to-PQL	35	Days from signup to PQL
Customers	50	33.3%	PQL-to-customer	15	Days from PQL to customer
Active customers 45	45	90.0%	active customers	120	Days to breakeven
				725	Average customer life (days)

13.2 Step 2: Defining PQLs

In the traditional customer acquisition process, marketing is in charge of generating and nurturing leads until they are ready to buy. This qualification process includes understanding a prospect's profile and company data, as well as responses to marketing such as downloading a whitepaper, opening an e-mail, or attending a webinar. As we highlighted earlier, such engagement is minimally correlated with buying intent, which is why we see a low MQL-to-customer conversion rate.

In additional to a prospect's profile and company data, PQL also includes in-product behavioral data to quantify buying intent. There are three categories of data that define PQL state: profile, company data, and CBI. CBI is an essential aspect of a product-led strategy, as it provides insights into customer intent and predicts how likely a user is to progress to the next stage of the customer lifecycle. So, essentially:

PQL = profile + company + CBI

In some cases, companies can break down PQLs into more granular milestones. As we showed in Chapter 9, at Aptrinsic, the process of getting a prospect to the PQL stage includes four milestones. Each milestone represents the completion of a certain onboarding journey.

Figure 13.1 - The Definition of PQL

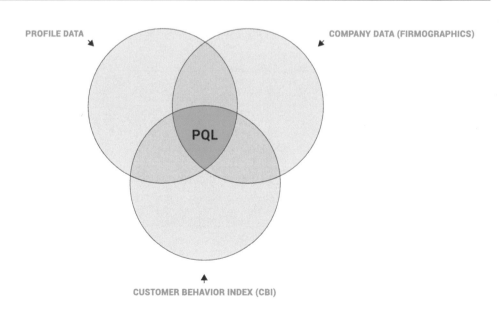

1. Profile Data

Profile data includes a prospect's name, e-mail, title, function, and sometimes other information.

2. Company (or firmographic data)

Company data includes company name, size, industry, revenue, location, news, and other relevant company-related details.

3. CBI

Companies are familiar with profile and company data since both are a part of the traditional sales funnel. The CBI introduces a new concept for measuring and understanding how engaged prospects and customers are with the product.

Step 3: Understanding the CBI

The CBI is a metric (often normalized) that measures how engaged your prospects and customers are, based on their in-product activity and usage.

CBI measures user engagement through the whole customer lifecycle. By incorporating a CBI into their product-led strategy, companies can predict adoption, retention, and growth of a customer. A CBI calculation includes all the usage and interactions that a user has with the product. These are weighted by how much a specific interaction is correlated with the likelihood of a customer advancing to the next stage of the customer lifecycle. Ultimately, they are correlated with CLV.

CBI includes, but is not limited to, the following metrics:

- DAU/MAU, or the number of logins over a period of time
- Average time spent in-product per session
- Number of completed core use cases
- Number of features interacted with
- Engagements with in-product notifications

CBI enables teams to anticipate issues that customers may run into, and use that insight to design behavior-based triggers that automate engagement for appropriate situations.

13.3 Step 4: Monitoring Customer Satisfaction

Customer satisfaction metrics show how engaged customers are, how much value they derived from your product, and whether they will recommend your solution to peers. Customer satisfaction reflects how a customer perceives the value and experience with your company, brand, and product. A few examples of metrics in this category include NPS, CBI, and CLV.

- CBI helps you figure out how, and how often, customers interact with your product.
- NPS helps you determine how likely a customer is to recommend your product.
- CLV helps you understand the potential net profit over the entire future relationship with a customer.

Even though your product is a SaaS offering, there are real costs associated with migration, integration, and training. While sales teams are typically focused on minimizing those costs to get new accounts signed on, the reality is that customer success teams should emphasize those switching costs[3]. Remember: the goal is to retain the customer by providing as much product value as possible, and making a switch seem unappealing.

Let's not forget that your customers will likely be judging their experience of your product based on their experience with best-in-class apps and leading consumer companies (i.e., the industry standard-bearers). It's critical to understand which of these aspects and features your customers most value and appreciate so you understand how the customer experience with your product is being measured.

A product-led strategy enables companies to measure customer satisfaction more accurately through both self-reported surveys and behavioral data. Furthermore, personalizing the customer experience based on in-product behaviors gives users more reasons to stay with your product.

There are a few reasons why customers can use your product and not be satisfied. Remember: the decision to sign on to use your product wasn't necessarily unanimous. Perhaps it was pushed through because of an executive's ties to the leadership of your company. Regardless, your goal is to make all the users happy with the decision so you reduce the likelihood of churn.

Even though your product is a SaaS offering, there are real costs associated with migration, integration, and training. While sales teams are typically focused on minimizing those costs to get new accounts signed on, the reality is that customer success teams should emphasize those switching costs. Remember: the goal is to retain the customer by providing as much product value as possible, and making a switch seem unappealing.

Let's not forget that your customers will likely be judging their experience of your product based on their experience with best-in-class apps and leading consumer companies (i.e., the industry standard-bearers). It's critical to understand which of these aspects and features your customers most value and appreciate so you understand how the customer experience with your product is being measured.

A product-led strategy enables companies to measure customer satisfaction more accurately through both self-reported surveys and behavioral data. Furthermore, personalizing the customer experience based on in-product behaviors gives users more reasons to stay with your product.

Your organization needs to keep a finger on the pulse of customer experience and satisfaction, and identify the customers who are using your product but aren't happy with it. Customers who get stuck with a bad experience when using your product can negatively impact your brand. Even if they haven't churned yet, they might share their dissatisfaction on social media or through other venues, and influence buying decisions in their extended networks. If you've spent time on LinkedIn, you've probably seen someone asking for a product review or complaining about the product they are using; and you know such discussions can quickly catch fire and go viral.

Asking customers why they feel a certain way may not yield real answers. In fact, people are shown to lie quite frequently when surveyed[4]. The reasons for their lies can include a desire for self-preservation (for example, wanting to appear better than they are), and to be helpful by giving what they think are the desirable answers; or they can believe their answers are correct, but it's hard to be certain when trying to recall a moment from long ago or envision a future scenario. Plus, the outcomes and perceptions of many interactions can't be easily understood and analyzed by conducting surveys.

The NPS is a great tool to get an idea of overall customer satisfaction, but it's not good at diagnosing the problem. That said, it is still valuable for assessing the customer experience. Even experienced teams sometimes overlook this metric, but it can be an early diagnostic tool to predict how churn rate will change in the future[5].

Another option is to observe users in their "natural habitat" (i.e., their work environment) as they use your product. Watching how a sample of users interact with your product can quickly yield valuable insights. However, this may not be very practical or scalable to do with each new feature release.

TIPS:
- Beware of written surveys. Occasionally conduct phone or in-person interviews.
- Never ask "What don't you like?" about your product or competitor,
  because people don't want to admit that they made a mistake.

Customer health (or customer satisfaction) should be evaluated based not only on self-reported surveys such as the NPS score, but also based on customer behaviors. Customer behavior is a more reliable metric than answers provided on self-reported surveys. That's because people can't always remember—or remember accurately—what their experience was like once they're outside of it. In many instances, customer behavior is all that matters. A properly designed and executed product-led strategy should enable the company to calculate CBI to predict customer satisfaction and retention.

Customer Health (Satisfaction) = CBI + NPS

13.4 Step 5: Analyzing Product Engagement and Adoption Metrics

What has been missing from the traditional customer acquisition process is product usage and feature adoption metrics. Customer satisfaction metrics assess how effective companies are in engaging and delivering value to customers. The product-led strategy adds a new dimension by analyzing product features, core use cases, and other product usage metrics to decide what to build next, what feature to discontinue, or what customer journey needs to be redesigned.

Here are a few examples of product engagement and adoption metrics that a company should consider:

- Percentage of users that use a particular product feature or channel (for example, InVision can track the percentage of customers that use a mobile app on a daily or monthly basis)
- Number of steps or clicks it takes a customer to complete core product use cases (for example, for Expensify, it could be the number of steps or clicks it takes to file and approve an expense report)
- Average time it takes for a user to complete core product journeys (for example, at Aptrinsic, we track how long it takes prospects to implement our JS code in their products)
- Percentage of users or sessions where the number of steps or clicks exceed the optimal

number (for example, MailChimp can track the percentage of customers that exceed the optimal—smallest—number of clicks it takes to create an e-mail marketing campaign)
- Average number of days it takes a newly signed-up prospect to fully onboard with the product (for example, Asana can track the average number of days it takes for a new user to create the project, assign tasks, and complete 10 tasks)

The successful product-led strategy enables teams to understand what product features are driving adoption and engagement, and for which customer segment. This data helps evaluate the product on a deeper level when used in combination with customer satisfaction metrics (NPS and CBI). Contrast this with the traditional GTM strategy, where the granular breakdown of product usage data is missing from the customer acquisition process. As a result, marketing teams rarely segment customers based on product usage and features and instead use outside-of-the-product interaction data to optimize lead generation campaigns. In other words, with the traditional model, the best the organization can do is use demographics and outside of the product data to impact marketing campaigns.

13.5 Step 6: Measuring Core Business Metrics

A few vital SaaS metrics are used to assess the health of a SaaS company. Aside from the basic revenue growth metrics, such as MRR and annual recurring revenue (ARR), SaaS teams need to closely monitor CLV, CAC, average selling price, and break-even.

Let's review these core SaaS metrics and how they are influenced by a product-led approach.

Customer Lifetime Value (CLV) is a prediction of the net profit attributable to the entire future relationship with a customer. It is the revenue generated from customers between the time the company reaches the break-even point with them and the end of the relationship with them.

Customer Acquisition Cost (CAC) is the average amount that a company spends to acquire a single customer. CAC is the sum of all customer acquisition costs, including sales & marketing expenses and salaries divided by the number of customers acquired during the same period.

Average Selling Price (ASP) is the amount of revenue per customer generated.

Break-even is a point when a company generates enough revenue from a customer to cover all the costs and expenses it took to acquire this customer.

Customer Lifetime Value as a core metric

Every SaaS organization should strive toward increasing CLV, because it closely correlates to the value a company provides to a customer. It also correlates to the company's profitability. The longer a SaaS company can keep a subscribed customer by providing value, the more profitable it is.

SaaS businesses can calculate CLV in a few ways. The most common way is to multiply average revenue per account (ARPA) by customer lifespan. (You can find more details in this infographic by Kissmetrics[6].) However, this calculation doesn't consider the average CAC. Another common CLV calculation is average MRR x gross margin x customer lifetime in months. (Check out this great guide to SaaS metrics by Eckhard Ortwein for more details[7]).

What is common among all traditional CLV calculations is that they use grossly simplified average numbers and, because of this, are not useful for predicting CLV trends early. Since it takes time for companies to evaluate new gross margins or ARPA, they cannot respond in a timely way to trends around changing CLV values.

The properly executed product-led strategy can help teams not only segment customers and forecast CLV for each segment, but also predict the rise and fall of CLV value based on in-product customer behaviors. For example, let's say last month your marketing team generated 1,000 product signups. However, after the first month, the CBI for this group is below average, which will result in a lower than expected signup-to-customer conversion rate. Your team can forecast how your CLV will change based on this data and can adjust current campaigns to improve the quality of signups and likelihood of conversion.

A successful product-led GTM strategy is not just about providing a freemium or free trial; it is a strategic way of increasing virality and reducing CAC.

Monitoring CLV vs CAC ratio and breakeven analysis

The ratio between CLV and CAC shows how effective and efficient a company is in acquiring, retaining, and growing its customers. No business can sustain a CLV-to-CAC ratio below one in the long term. Such a ratio means the company spends more money to acquire a customer than the revenue it generates from the customer. As David Skok pointed out in his article "**STARTUP KILLER: THE COST OF CUSTOMER ACQUISITION**"[8], an unhealthy CLV-to-CAC ratio could very well signal the end of your company. A healthy CLV-to-CAC ratio, Skok explains, is when CLV is three times or more greater than CAC.

If the CAC is higher than CLV, the company is either paying too much for customers or doesn't provide enough value to retain them—or both. Calculating expected CAC and CLV—as Tomasz Tunguz explains how to do in his article, "**THE MATH BEHIND SAAS STARTUP CUSTOMER LIFETIME VALUE**"[9]—can provide a more accurate view.

Before a prospect becomes a customer, a company accumulates costs. The purchasing event then triggers the process of recovering this customer acquisition investment. At this stage, the customer is moving toward the break-even point, which means generating revenue to cover all CAC. With a product-led strategy, companies can reduce the customer acquisition cost by building virality into freemium and free trial offerings. When existing users invite others to try your product, you avoid the need to spend money trying to acquire a new customer through traditional channels.

The value doesn't end there. A product-led strategy also helps companies understand what customer journeys, product features, and usage patterns influence average selling prices and the time it takes to reach the break-even point. With these insights, they can design their products, campaigns and communications to shorten the time to reach break-even, while also commanding higher average selling prices.

That said, companies should not only think about optimizing CLV to minimize their costs. This is according to Michael Schrage, the author of **WHO DO YOU WANT YOUR CUSTOMERS TO BECOME?**[10] As he highlighted in his article "**WHAT MOST COMPANIES MISS ABOUT CUSTOMER LIFETIME VALUE**"[11], by focusing on how to provide and extract maximum value to customers, companies can improve CLV in a way that benefits them in more and more meaningful, ways. For example, customers can suggest new product features and evangelize about companies and products on social media channels. They can even introduce your product to new customers and provide early feedback on a new product release or feature. In other words, by asking who you want your customers to become and what makes your customers more valuable, you can take a different perspective of CLV. In fact, you can measure it differently.

The product-led strategy fits the notion, described by Michael Schrage, of evaluating innovation and product investments based on what behaviors you want your customers to exhibit. Done successfully, this enables your company to design shorter and more agile feedback loops to build a product that your customers will love.

The table below summarizes the core metrics for a SaaS company using a product-led GTM strategy.

Table 13.5 - Essential SaaS Metrics

Customer Lifecycle	Effectiveness Metrics	Velocity Metrics
• Visits • Signups • PQLs • Customers • Active Customers • Renewed/retained • Churned	• Visits-to-Signup Rate • Signup-to-PQL Rate • PQL-to-Customer Rate • Signup-to-Customer Rate • Customer Churn Rate • MRR Churn Rate • MRR Expansion Rate • Net MRR Churn	• Days from signup to PQL • Days from PQL to customer • Days from signup to customer • Days to break-even • Average Customer Life
Customer Health Metrics	**Product Adoption Metrics**	**Core Business Metrics**
• CBI • NPS	• DAU / MAU • % of users using feature • Number of steps for core journeys • Average time to complete core journey • Average number of days for new signup to get fully onboarded	• CLV • CAC • ASP • CLV to CAC ratio • Break-even

The diagram below summarizes customer states in a lifecycle, and critical metrics to evaluate the performance of a SaaS company using a product-led GTM approach.

Figure 13.2 - Essential SaaS Metrics

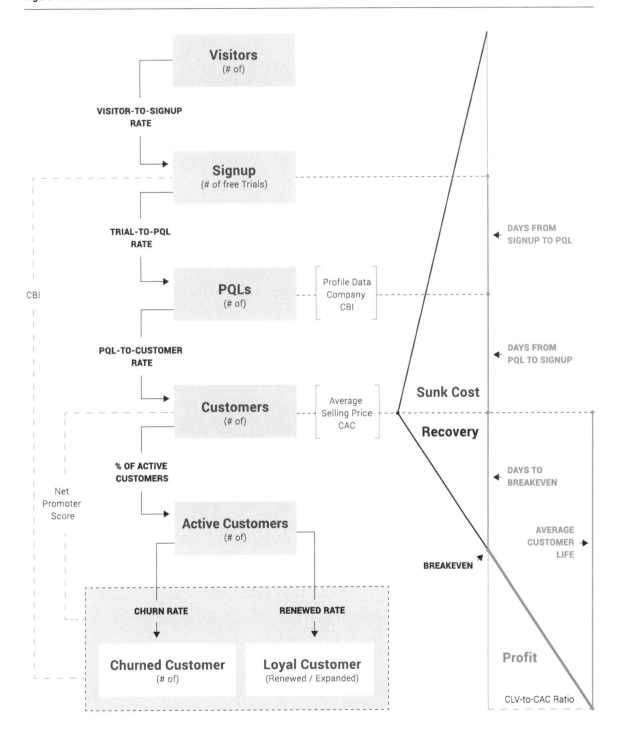

13.6 Key Takeaways

- A product-led strategy changes how companies track the effectiveness of customers moving through different lifecycle stages.
- Measuring the conversion rate from one state to the next helps companies understand what part of the lifecycle can be improved.
- With a product-led approach, there are seven states in the customer lifecycle:
  1. Visitor
  2. Signup/Trial
  3. PQL
  4. Customer
  5. Active Customer
  6. Renewed/Retained
  7. Churned
- A high churn rate can put a SaaS company out of business.
- Velocity metrics describe how long it takes a company to achieve certain milestones.
- The CBI is the essential (often normalized) metric for a product-led strategy. It measures how engaged your prospects and customers are based on their in-product activity and usage.
- Customer satisfaction metrics show how engaged customers are, how much value they derive from your product, and whether they recommend your solution to peers.
- Customer health (or customer satisfaction) should be evaluated based not only on self-reported surveys such as NPS scores, but also analyzed based on customer behaviors. A product-led strategy enables companies to measure in this way.
- Customers that are stuck using your product can negatively impact your brand.
- A product-led strategy brings a new dimension by analyzing product features, core use cases, and other product usage metrics to decide what to build next, what feature to discontinue, and/or what customer journey needs a redesign.
- Aside from basic revenue growth metrics, such as MRR and ARR, SaaS teams need to closely monitor CLV, CAC, ASP, and break-even.
- Focus on maximizing CLV both by delivering maximum value to customers and extracting maximum value from them.

Chapter 14
Three Pillars That Support a Successful Product-Led GTM Strategy

A product-led GTM strategy provides a new framework for how leading SaaS organizations think about taking products to market and acquiring, retaining, and growing customers in a repeatable, scalable way.

Top management must get behind this approach to ensure the whole organization is supporting personalized customer experiences. We've discussed a few ways that product-led strategy enables companies to focus on personalized customer experiences. Let's cover three pillars that are essential to delivering these experiences:

- Data & Analytics
- Engagement Capability
- Experimentation

But first, answer these questions:

Can your organization track, integrate, and analyze comprehensive customer profile and behavioral data?

Can your organization create automated and near-real-time, omnichannel engagements based on available customer data?

Can your organization experiment with product features, messages, and engagements in a timely manner with minimal risk?

If you answered "no" to one or more of these questions, it's critical that you put in place the following elements to support your product-led GTM strategy.

Figure 14.1 - The Three Pillars of a Product-Led GTM Strategy

14.1 Pillar #1: Data & Analytics

According to the 2016 "Businesses @ Work" report by Okta[1], an average organi-zation uses 13 cloud applications. Many of these cloud solutions create or store customer profile and/or behavioral data. At the same time, most organizations still rely on a combination of on-premise and cloud-based applications to capture and store this information (such as CRM, marketing automation, customer support, and customer success solutions). The challenge for many organizations is to aggregate customer data across all systems of record, no matter where they reside.

It's not about dumping all available data into one data warehouse. It is not enough to know that a user with a certain e-mail logged into your product. Teams should also be aware, for example, of how much a customer is paying, as well as how many team members are using the product and the number of open support tickets attached to the account.

The cornerstone of a successful product-led strategy is understanding:

- Holistic customer experiences
- Where they are in their customer lifecycle
- What journeys have been completed
- Details about customer experiences across multiple interactions

Comprehensive customer data should include customer profile data (demo-graphics), customer behavioral data, and production data. When it comes to this data, it must be comprehensive, intelligent, timely, and actionable. Let's explain what we mean by each of these.

Comprehensive

Does our data tell us about every experience that a customer has with our company, brand, and product?

Intelligent

Does our data answer important business questions, and have we analyzed it for meaning?

Timely (a.k.a. Real Time)

How quickly is this data collected and analyzed to enable us to respond to individual customers, as well as see market trends in their early stages?

Actionable

Can we create contextual engagements with individual customers in a timely manner based on our data?

We have discussed the importance of understanding your customers by developing a 360-degree view of them; but often, organizations are stuck with what we call "forensic data"—data collected long after the fact and not comprehensive or actionable.

Let's use a real-world example that highlights the importance of providing product managers with unified customer data. We won't name the company, but this story was shared with our team as we interviewed product managers.

In this company, over 50 percent of customer success and customer support issues were related to a single problematic product feature. Because the company was dedicating so many resources across departments to support this feature, the company wondered whether it was better to remove it from the product. To make this decision, the product manager had to estimate the potential impact on customers and revenue. Specifically, the company needed to figure out which customers used this feature, how often, and the combined revenue of customers using the feature. Then it could decide which customers could be lost with minimal impact to overall revenues. This analysis proved to be difficult.

The manager had to match product usage data from a product analytics solution with customer/account data from a CRM system. That took a couple of days. Then, he had to answer a list of questions (i.e., which customers used this feature, how often, and so on) to determine how much revenue was associated with a particular feature.

Ideally, your product manager could handle this exercise much more efficiently. Your data management and analytics system should be able to answer how many prospects signed up today and failed to complete a journey to realize initial value.

14.2 Pillar #2: Engagement Engine

Data and analytics are not enough to personalize customer experiences. Your company needs the tools and capability to act on data in a timely manner. The cost of delayed customer engagement is the loss of context and customer interest. Here are two tactics to improve the effectiveness of customer engagement: automating personalized engagement, and omnichannel engagement delivery.

Automating engagements

Automating customer engagements with behavioral-based triggers can help teams shorten response times and ensure contextual engagements (the right customer at the right time with the right message via the right channel). If your customer and product data and segmentation are housed in one place, you can call upon a single system (i.e., engagement engine) to act on this data. This enables you to create engagement and respond quickly to behavior-based triggers. An example would be reminding someone via e-mail to log in to your app when they haven't done so within a set period of time.

Omnichannel experience

Omnichannel experience is a critical part the new customer experience era. Not only do products need to be experienced consistently across multiple devices, communication with prospects and customers—from in-product notification to e-mail reminders—has to be smooth across all channels including mobile apps.

The following are two common challenges to creating effective omnichannel engagement:

Efficiency: Can the organization create one engagement campaign and deliver it simultaneously across multiple channels?

Consistency: Do your customers have consistent experiences when they engage with your campaigns or messages?

Here's an example of consistency: Let's say a customer dropped out of a journey on a desktop browser. Your campaign should bring that person back to complete the journey the same place they left off, whether they rejoin using a desktop browser or a mobile app.

14.3 Pillar #3: Experimentation

Colonel Tom Kolditz, professor and head of the Department of Behavioral Sciences and Leadership at the U.S. Military Academy, said that no plan survives contact with the enemy. When it comes to the personalized customer experience you deliver as part of your product-led approach, customers can be very unpredictable and unforgiving. The key is to be proactive and quickly respond to customer behaviors and changing needs.

Companies that learn from their customers and iterate fast will be more successful than those that don't. That's why experimentation has become mandatory in a SaaS environment. But experimentation is not just about conducting one-off A/B tests. Your company needs to conduct experiments on a large scale, and in more automated ways. For example, you could create onboarding experiences for three or four customer segments and test each newly signed-up customer in real time, and adjust your onboarding flows accordingly.

A product-led GTM strategy is the most effective way for your company to deliver the personalized customer experiences that are essential for long-term growth and success. An effective product-led strategy hinges on the ability to assemble and manage a 360-degree view of your customers' data, engage in real time consistently on all channels, and experiment at scale to accelerate how you learn and adapt to customer needs.

Chapter 15
Conclusion: The Future of SaaS is the Personalized Product Experience

It should come as no surprise that digital transformation is impacting every aspect of our society. In this book, we are guilty of referencing some of the most overused examples, such as Amazon and Netflix, to explain the force behind this transformation. But that's because most of us can relate to how the customer experience has changed because of these visionaries.

What if your company could join their ranks by delivering such memorable customer experiences? It's possible that you've been trying to figure out just how to do that. But like many other businesses, we bet you've been going about it the wrong way. The right way—the way that is proving effective for the newest generation of SaaS companies—is to embrace the product-led approach and philosophy we've outlined in this book.

You can argue that new technologies have enabled the incredible growth trajectories of companies like Uber and Airbnb, but when you drill down, it becomes obvious that customer experience is what fuels such rapid growths. Uber did not make a better dispatch for taxis; Uber reinvented the entire process of getting from one place to another. Airbnb did not make it easier or more convenient to book hotels; it reinvented the whole travel experience.

A similar transformation happened in the enterprise software industry when companies began offering their software via the cloud, but today, the SaaS business model is par for the course. To stand apart, SaaS companies must do more than provide more features and lower prices. They must understand how their products solve customer needs and change processes. Just as importantly, they must understand how to satisfy customer expectations for an Amazon-like experience. Welcome to the customer experience era!

Designing for the customer experience is crucial to your success as a SaaS company, but the first step is putting your organization in the shoes of those that buy your product. That means your sales marketing team, sales team, customer success team, and even your product team must understand what your customers are trying to achieve, how they buy, and what experience they want from your product.

Arriving at this understanding is essential, and it needs to happen before you do anything else— before you create any marketing content, design your sales process, outline your customer success operations, or develop all your product features.

Do this well, and your company will transform to become truly customer-focused, truly experience-driven, and truly product-led. It will focus more on overall customer journeys than on individual interactions; more on the customer lifecycle than the sales funnel; and more on the end-to-end customer experience and CLV than on individual department goals and the size of the deal.

If there is one idea that we want you to take from this book it is this: Delivering a personalized customer experience is critical for your survival, and the transition to a product-led GTM gives your organization the best chance to succeed.

A product-led GTM is proving to be a better alternative than the traditional customer acquisition approach. Many of today's fastest-growing enterprise software companies are implementing product-led GTM strategies. We named a few of them throughout this book: Slack, Zoom, Asana, InVision, Expensify, and Dropbox. These companies realized that nothing is more valuable than understanding how customers use, interact with, and feel about their products. Not even NPS and customer satisfaction surveys can provide as much insight as actually monitoring and analyzing how customers interact with your product and service in the real world.

That's why Google doesn't ask you how it can improve its search capabilities. Instead, it monitors billions of searches—and your specific requests—to improve the search results.

That's why Facebook ignored the outrage against News Feed when it was first introduced in 2006. Despite the uproar, data showed that users viewed 10 billion more pages just two months after the feature was introduced.

That's why Netflix doesn't ask its customers what movies and shows they want to watch. Instead, Netflix recommends shows based on your prior behavior, and the preferences of people with similar tastes.

The insight that companies can extract by analyzing how prospects and customers use their product is by far the most important element of building a highly successful company. We are not advocating against the use NPS and customer surveys. We are simply arguing that product behavioral data uncovers more insights faster, and is the cornerstone of delivering a great customer experience.

It's no longer enough for a SaaS company to know the demographics of its target customers.

In-product behavioral data is the key, and a product-led GTM strategy wrapped around a freemium or free trial enables SaaS companies to collect this data sooner in the buying process.

That said, to succeed with a product-led GTM strategy, SaaS companies must do more than simply provide a freemium or free trial. They must embrace an organization-wide strategic mindset that enables their teams to get prospects using the product early in the customer acquisition process, and then guide them through their in-product journeys. To achieve that goal, SaaS companies must do three things:

- Assemble unified customer profile data (including in-depth product usage data)
- Invest in tools that enable near-real-time customer engagement
- Design experiments that yield deep and continual insights

Freemium and free trials can certainly increase the virality of your product and reduce CAC. However, without focusing on behavioral-driven product adoption, the cost of providing a free offering almost certainly outweighs the benefits. That is why so many companies still stick with lead forms and gated free trials that require a sales touch. These organizations know that their processes and approach weren't built to enable a product-led strategy. As a result, they can't profitably guide prospects in-product before they are ready for a conversation with a sales team.

As SaaS companies transition to a product-led GTM strategy, the role of product leaders will expand. Product managers will become part of the customer acquisition process, and will need to build agile operations to help their organizations succeed in a dynamic market. The pressure to build the right features and processes will force product managers to pay increasingly more attention to behavioral data.

Product adoption is a continuous process. It never stops, just as there is no final destination to an excellent product experience. Technologies improve quickly and they push the standard further. More product leaders will be responsible not only for product experience, NPS and satisfaction scores, but also for growing customer lifetime values and reducing signup-to-customer rates by enabling quicker time to value and excellent onboarding.

We've already seen how sales organizations had to adapt during the sales-led era of early SaaS, and how marketing automation shifted organizations to a marketing-led approach. Now, with a product-led approach, we are witnessing how product organizations will need to adapt to shoulder growing responsibility for customer experiences and the acquisition process.

Every few years, we hear about new sales or marketing tactics such as content marketing, demand generation, social selling, or account-based sales and marketing. Our intent is not to contribute to the noise. Whether the industry will ever use the term "product-qualified lead," or whether or not a "product-led GTM strategy" becomes the new industry standard. is not the point.

Regardless of nomenclature, in the next decade, product will be the primary tool enterprise software vendors use to create compelling customer experiences. The next wave of successful software companies will use their product to monitor and engage prospects and customers contextually. By doing so, they will deliver the experiences required to succeed in the customer experience era.

Frankly, we don't know if people will start hiring "customer lifecycle managers" to oversee customer experience, or whether product teams will assign "product operations managers" to manage unified data sources, product engagement, and experimentation tools; but we are willing to bet that the forces behind rising customer expectations will yield very big and meaningful changes.

You can be sure that machine learning and Artificial Intelligence (AI) will enable the next generation of software companies to better predict future customer behavior and act on this data in a real-time, omnichannel, and automated way. Why shouldn't we expect SaaS companies to learn and adapt to our goals and preferences? If Amazon and Netflix can do it, so can any other company. The AI revolution promises to enhance our experiences and make them more personal and engaging.

In fact, these technologies, along with behavioral data generated via a product-led strategy, make it possible to more accurately predict the prospects most likely to convert and the customers most likely to renew and upgrade. In other words, it empowers SaaS companies to better predict prospects with the highest CLV potential, and take actions with customers to increase the likelihood of achieving that goal. Simply put, adding predictability to the equation enables SaaS companies to take their businesses to new heights faster than ever before.

The bottom line: Whoever is closest to the customer wins, and a product-led strategy puts companies closer to their customers than ever before. That said, every company is different and each product is unique, so no single process or prescription applies to every case.

Throughout this book we have outlined multiple ideas that could be helpful in your quest to deliver more personalized products and implement a product-led GTM strategy. Some ideas we covered in more detail than others. This book is just a starting point, and we hope to spark an ongoing discussion that will lead to deeper coverage of many concepts touched upon here. Please use these ideas as inspiration and a starting point—take what's useful, ignore what's not, and add anything that's unique to your product and company.

Let Us Hear from You

We are sharing this book free of charge. If you find it helpful, please share it on Facebook, Linkedin, Twitter, Quora, Reddit, and other platforms of your choice. We hope you will share this book with your team and share your own stories about what you have learned. We will add them to the next version of this book.

We encourage you to call upon this book to spark your own discussions and inspire your own blog posts and other content. Please just remember to reference our work.

We are also starting a discussion on how to personalize product experiences with a product-led GTM strategy. Please tweet your questions to @aptrinsic (twitter.com/aptrinsic) and leave comments on Medium, where this full book is available (goo.gl/3nqRMc).

Try not to lose, and keep it SaaSy!

Thank you for reading our book. Now go forth and master the product experience!

Fun Facts About This Book
- 90-ish references
- 50k-ish words
- 19 figures
- 16 tables

Acknowledgements

Writing a book has proven to be a daunting challenge of research, writing, revisions, and updates. We have referenced more than 90 articles, books, and research items in the book, based on more than 300 articles, books, interviews and other content that we read and analyzed over several months. We would like to thank everyone who contributed to this wealth of publicly available knowledge. That's why we are sharing this book online for free. We don't even ask for your e-mail address; as we discussed in this book, we don't believe in lead forms.

We also say thank you to everyone who was in some way involved in creating this book. Especially, we would like to thank our small but very dynamic team at Aptrinsic.

EDITORS: Steve Schaefer, Stephanie Tilton
DESIGNER AND ILLUSTRATOR: Verena Tam

WE WERE INSPIRED BY CONTENT CREATED BY THESE INDUSTRY EXPERTS:
David Skok, Tom Tunguz, Lincoln Murphy, Jason Lemkin, Tae Hea Nahm, Al Ramadan

SPECIAL THANKS FOR PROVIDING FEEDBACK AND HELP CREATING THIS BOOK:
Dan Avida, Tom Wentworth, Travis Kaufman, Bill Portelli, Robert Tinker, Aleh Haiko, Marissa Bonfiglio, Erick Mott, Mikita Mikado, David Schlossberg, Phil Fernandez, Lauren Smiley, David Lassen

LIST OF COMPANIES MENTIONED IN THIS BOOK: Amazon, Netflix, Linkedin, Airbnb, eSurance, Salesforce, Marketo, Hubspot, Apttus, Slack, Invision, Asana, Zoom.us, Dropbox, Trello, Atlassian, Zendesk, Splunk, Expensify, Pandadoc, Mailchimp, Rapidminer

References

Partial Bibliography
This book was inspired by many books, including these:

Beckwith, Harry. **SELLING THE INVISIBLE: A FIELD GUIDE TO MODERN MARKETING.**
New York: Grand Central, 2012. Print.

Blank, Steve. **THE STARTUP OWNER'S MANUAL: THE STEP-BY-STEP GUIDE FOR BUILDING A GREAT COMPANY.** Cork: BookBaby, 2012. Print.

Bradley, Stephen P., and Richard L. Nolan. **SENSE & RESPOND: CAPTURING VALUE IN THE NETWORK ERA.** Boston, Mass: Harvard Business School, 1998. N. pag. Print.

Drucker, Peter Ferdinand. **THE ESSENTIAL DRUCKER SELECTIONS FROM THE MANAGEMENT WORKS.** London: Routledge, 2011. Print.

Jiwa, Bernadette. **MARKETING A LOVE STORY: HOW TO MATTER TO YOUR CUSTOMERS.** Charleston, SC: Story of Telling, 2015. Print.

Kooij, Jacco van der, and Fernando Pizarro. **BLUEPRINTS FOR A SAAS SALES ORGANIZATION.** Winning by Design, 2015.

Levitt, Theodore. **MARKETING IMAGINATION.** Sperling & Kupfer Editori, 1990.

Moore, Geoffrey. **CROSSING THE CHASM: MARKETING AND SELLING HIGH-TECH PRODUCTS TO MAINSTREAM CUSTOMERS.** New York: HarperCollins, 2014. Print.

Olsen, Dan. **THE LEAN PRODUCT PLAYBOOK: HOW TO INNOVATE WITH MINIMUM VIABLE PRODUCTS AND RAPID CUSTOMER FEEDBACK.** John Wiley & Sons, 2015.

Ramadan, Al, et al. **PLAY BIGGER: HOW PIRATES, DREAMERS, AND INNOVATORS CREATE AND DOMINATE MARKETS.** Harper Business, 2016.

Roberge, Mark. **THE SALES ACCELERATION FORMULA: USING DATA, TECHNOLOGY, AND INBOUND SELLING TO GO FROM $0 TO $100 MILLION.** Hoboken, NJ: Wiley, 2015. Print.

Schrage, Michael. **WHO DO YOU WANT YOUR CUSTOMERS TO BECOME?** Boston, Mass: Harvard Business School, 2012. Print.

Stephens-Davidowitz, Seth. **EVERYBODY LIES: WHAT THE INTERNET CAN TELL US ABOUT WHO WE REALLY ARE.** Bloomsbury, 2017.

Wheeler, Alina. **DESIGNING BRAND IDENTITY: A COMPLETE GUIDE TO CREATING, BUILDING, AND MAINTAINING STRONG BRANDS.** John Wiley, 2006.

Notes

Chapter 1

1. Pine, B. Joseph, and James H. Gilmore, "Welcome to the Experience Economy", Harvard Business Review, July-August 1998, https://hbr.org/1998/07/welcome-to-the-experience-economy.

2. Kriss, Peter, "The Value of Customer Experience, Quantified", Harvard Business Review, August 1, 2014, https://hbr.org/2014/08/the-value-of-customer-experience-quantified.

3. Bonnet, Didier, Jerome, Buvat, and Subrahmanyam KJV, "When Digital Disruption Strikes: How Can Incumbents Respond?", Capgemeni.com, February 23, 2015, https://www.capgemini.com/consulting/wp-content/uploads/sites/30/2017/07/digital_disruption_1.pdf.

4. Kaplan, Bonnie, et al, Information Systems Research: Relevant Theory and Informed Practice. Berlin/Heidelberg: Springer Science & Business Media, 2004). https://books.google.com/books?id=6fmSk7ykB2sC&pg=PA689.

5. "Borders Group >> Revenue", Wikiinvest, last modified Q4 2010, http://www.wikinvest.com/stock/Borders_Group_(BGP)/Data/Revenue.

6. Liedtkte, Michael, and Mae Anderson, "Blockbuster tries to rewrite script in bankruptcy", Associated Press, September 23, 2010, http://archive.boston.com/business/articles/2010/09/23/blockbuster_tries_to_rewrite_script_in_bankruptcy/.

7. Carr, Austin, "Blockbuster Bankruptcy: A Decade of Decline", Fast Company, September 22, 2010, https://www.fastcompany.com/1690654/blockbuster-bankruptcy-decade-decline.

8. Bernhard, Marchella, "Winner of the Week: Blockbuster", Forbes, March 30, 2001, https://www.forbes.com/forbes/welcome/?toURL=https://www.forbes.com/2001/03/30/0330winner.html&refURL=&referrer=.

9. "Netflix's annual revenue from 2002 to 2016 (in million U.S. dollars)", Statista, accessed October 2, 2017, https://www.statista.com/statistics/272545/annual-revenue-of-netflix/.

10. Jacobsohn, Sean, Aaron Levie, and Jeetu Patel, "Norwest Enterprise Cloud Leaders Forum", Vimeo, February 2, 2017, https://vimeo.com/200854092.

11. Lunden, Ingrid, "Randstad buys Monster for $429M as recruitment consolidation continues", TechCrunch, August 8, 2016, https://techcrunch.com/2016/08/08/randstad-buys-monster-for-429m-as-recruitment-consolidation-continues/.

12. Tully, Shawn, "Why Hotel Giant Marriott is on an Expansion Binge as It Fends Off Airbnb", Fortune, June 14, 2017, http://fortune.com/2017/06/14/marriott-arne-sorenson-starwood-acquisition-airbnb/.

13. Ibid.

14. Lawler, Ryan, "Airbnb Experiments with 'Experiences', Offering Everything From Bike Tours To Home-Cooked Meals", TechCrunch, May 16, 2014, https://techcrunch.com/2014/05/16/airbnb-experiences/.

15. Theobald, Stephanie, "Putting Aribnb's new hosted 'experience' to the test", The Guardian, December 4, 2016, https://www.theguardian.com/travel/2016/dec/04/airbnb-new-experiences-events.

16. Andreessen, Marc, "Why Software is Eating the World", The Wall Street Journal, August 20, 2011, http://www.aberdeeninvestment.com/wp-content/uploads/2009/11/Why-Software-Is-Eating-The-World-8-20-111.pdf.

17. Price, Bill, and David Jaffe, Your Customer Rules!: Delivering the Me2B Experiences That Today's Customers Demand (San Francisco: Jossey-Bass, 2014) https://www.amazon.com/gp/product/1118954777/.

18. Price, Bill, "Blurred Lines: Today's B2B Customers Expect B2C Experiences", Openview, May 21, 2015, http://labs.openviewpartners.com/bill-price-me2b-customer-experiences/#.WacdZneGOL5.

19. Tomasz Tunguz, "The Next Big Shift in SaaS", Tomasz Tunguz (blog), July 11, 2016, http://tomtunguz.com/from-displacer-to-disruptor/.

20. Lori Wizdo, "Accelerating Revenue In A Changed Economy", Forrester (blog), January 24, 2013, https://go.forrester.com/blogs/13-01-23-accelerating_revenue_in_a_changed_economy/.

21. Epstein, Caitlin, "Zoom Raises $30M in Series C Funding Led by Emergence Capital", Marketwired, February 4, 2015, http://www.marketwired.com/press-release/zoom-raises-30m-in-series-c-funding-led-by-emergence-capital-1988574.htm.

22. Bryan Kramer, "There is No More B2B or B2C: It's Human to Human, H2H", Bryan Kramer (blog), accessed October 2, 2017, http://www.bryankramer.com/there-is-no-more-b2b-or-b2c-its-human-to-human-h2h/.

23. Lingqvist, Oskar, Candace Lun Plotkin, and Jennifer Stanley, "Do you really understand how your business customers buy?", McKinsey Quarterly, February 2015, http://www.mckinsey.com/business-functions/marketing-and-sales/our-insights/do-you-really-understand-how-your-business-customers-buy.

Chapter 2

1. Harley Manning, "Customer Experience Defined", Forrester (blog), November 23, 2010, https://go.forrester.com/blogs/10-11-23-customer_experience_defined/.

2. Shankman, Samantha, "Interview: Hilton CEO on Being Everyting to Every Guest Everywhere", Skift, December 29, 2014, https://skift.com/2014/12/29/interview-hilton-ceo-on-being-everything-to-every-guest-everywhere/.

3. Grimes, Seth, "Airbnb, Travelocity, and Hilton Teach the Bad, Better, and Best of Net Promoter Surveys", CustomerThink, Juy 20, 2017, http://customerthink.com/airbnb-travelocity-and-hilton-teach-the-bad-better-and-best-of-net-promoter-surveys/.

4. Seth Brinker, "Marketing Technology Landscape Supergraphic (2017)", Chief Martec (blog), May 2017, http://chiefmartec.com/2017/05/marketing-techniology-landscape-supergraphic-2017/.

5. "Infographic: The Cost of Disappointed Customers", Thunderhead, accessed October 2017, https://www.thunderhead.com/useful-stuff/infographic-the-cost-of-disappointed-customers/.
6. Ibid.
7. Tornquist, Stefan, "The Consumer Conversation", eConstultancy, April 2015, https://econsultancy.com/reports/the-consumer-conversation/.
8. Steve Casey, "How Self-Service Research Will Change B2B Marketing", Forrester (blog), February 10, 2016, http://blogs.forrester.com/steve_casey/16-02-10-how_self_service_research_will_change_b2b_marketing.
9. "Customers want to help themselves?", Zendesk, accessed October 2, 2017, https://www.zendesk.com/resources/searching-for-self-service/.

Chapter 3
1. "The new charter for B2B marketing and sales in the age of the customer", Forrester, April 27, 2017, https://go.forrester.com/b2b-marketing-sales/.
2. Hoar, Andy, et al, "Death of a (B2B) Salesman), Forrester, April 13, 2015, https://www.forrester.com/report/Death+Of+A+B2B+Salesman/-/E-RES122288.
3. Finley, Klint, "Why Trello, a Simple To-Do Ap, is Worth $425 Million", Wired, January 9, 2017, https://www.wired.com/2017/01/trello-simple-app-worth-425-million-dollars/.

Chapter 4
1. "Product Lifecycles", Lumen Learning, accessed October 2nd, 2017, https://www.boundless.com/marketing/textbooks/boundless-marketing-textbook/products-9/product-life-cycles-69/impact-of-the-product-life-cycle-on-marketing-strategy-348-10771/.
2. Jenkins, Jon, "Velocity Culture", O'Reilly Publishing, June 20, 2011, https://www.youtube.com/watch?v=dxk8b9rSKOo.
3. Myk Pono, "How to Track Customer Acquisitions: Customer Lifecycle, Sales Funnel, and Content Strategy", Intrinsic Point (blog), June 1, 2016, https://intrinsicpoint.com/how-to-track-customer-acquisition-9d04b903535.

Chapter 5
1. Maechler, Nicolas, Kevin Neher, and Robert Park, "From touchpoints to journeys: Seeing the world as customers do", McKinsey Quarterly, March 2016, http://www.mckinsey.com/business-functions/marketing-and-sales/our-insights/from-touchpoints-to-journeys-seeing-the-world-as-customers-do.
2. Executive briefing, "The CEO Guide to customer experience", McKinsey Quarterly, August 2016, http://www.mckinsey.com/business-functions/operations/our-insights/the-ceo-guide-to-customer-experience.
3. Lincoln Murphy, "Understanding Your Customer's Desired Outcome", Sixteen Ventures (blog), accessed October 2, 2017, http://sixteenventures.com/customer-success-desired-outcome.

Chapter 6

1. Mark Roberge, "How Sales Comp Plans Impact Customer Churn", Thinkgrowth (blog), February 7 2017 https://thinkgrowth.org/how-sales-comp-plans-impact-customer-churn-23a15ecad5ef.

2. Robin Dechant, "7 Reasons why Product Management continues to play a greater role in SaaS", Point Nine Land (blog), April 19, 2017, https://medium.com/point-nine-news/7-reasons-why-product-management-continues-to-play-a-greater-role-in-SaaS-1e558f944f44.

3. Rouse, Margaret, "shadowIT", TechTarget, October 2012, http://searchcloudcomputing.techtarget.com/definition/shadow-IT-shadow-information-technology.

4. Roberge, Thinkgrowth February 2017.

Chapter 7

1. Currier, James, "Evolution of Channels", Ooga Labs, accessed October 2, 2017, https://static1.squarespace.com/static/528c45f9e4b06be250a9fe30/t/541d9a84e4b04cb5faeded 2f/1411226245303/growth-channels-james-currier?format=750w.

2. Minogue, Ashley, "Why You Should Sell to Users, Not Buyers: A Product-Led Approach to Marketing", Openview, May 16, 2017, http://labs.openviewpartners.com/product-led-growth-marketing-strategies/#.WaBpJneGNp9.

3. Diggins, Natalie, "Product-Led Growth: Strategies from Slack & Expensify", Openview, August 17 2016, http://labs.openviewpartners.com/product-led-growth/#.WaBpXneGNp9.

4. Nanji, Ayaz, "Conversion Benchmarks for Seven Types of Online Forms", MarketingProfs, March 25, 2015, http://www.marketingprofs.com/charts/2015/27318/conversion-benchmarks-for-seven-types-of-online-forms.

5. Tom Wentworth, "Why I'm Killing the Marketing Qualified Lead", Views from the 6(17), (blog), May 17, 2016, https://tomwentworth.com/why-im-killing-the-marketing-qualified-lead-95c90874bc6f.

6. Nahm, Tae Hea, "Attacking with Thought Leadership", Storm Ventures (blog), April 5, 2017, https://blog.stormventures.com/attacking-with-thought-leadership-6e38ac7490fb.

7. Tomasz Tunguz, "The Product Qualified Lead (PQL)", Tomasz Tunguz (blog), January 15, 2013, http://tomtunguz.com/the-new-sales-hotness-the-product-qualified-lead-pql/.

8. "Amazon's Friction-Killing Tactics to Make Products More Seamless", First Round Review, accessed October 2, 2017, http://firstround.com/review/amazons-friction-killing-tactics-to-make-products-more-seamless/.

9. Skala, Emmauelle, "Marketing Qualified Leads Are Cool, But I'll Take Product Qualified Leads Any Day", Sales Hacker, April 24, 2017, https://www.saleshacker.com/marketing-qualified-leads-product-qualified-leads/.

10. O'Donnell, Christopher, "Why Product Qualified Leads are the Answer to a Failing Freemium Model", Openview, April 19, 2016, https://expand.openviewpartners.com/what-is-a-pql-3d724548ba06.

11.

12. "IDC: Dropbox is the fastest SaaS company to reach $1 billion in revenue run rate", Dropbox (press release), February 2, 2017, https://www.dropbox.com/news/business/idc--dropbox-the-fastest-SaaS-company-to-reach--1-billion-in-rev.

Chapter 8

1. Lauren Seymour, "The seven-step go-to-market strategy", MaRS (blog), February 5, 2013, https://www.marsdd.com/news-and-insights/the-seven-step-go-to-market-strategy/.
2. Griffin, Tren, "12 Things about Product-Market Fit", Andreessen Horowitz, February 18, 2017, https://a16z.com/2017/02/18/12-things-about-product-market-fit/.
3. Jorgenson, Eric, "Product/Market Fit: What it really means, how to measure it, and where to find it", Evergreen Business Weekly, June 1, 2015, https://medium.com/evergreen-business-weekly/product-market-fit-what-it-really-means-how-to-measure-it-and-where-to-find-it-70e746be907b.
4. Myk Pono, "Strategic Communication: How to Develop Strategic Messaging and Positioning", Intrinsic Point (blog), December 14, 2016, https://intrinsicpoint.com/strategic-communication-how-to-develop-strategic-messaging-and-positioning-3cc59689ca28.

Chapter 9

1. Lemkin, Jason, "Why You Need 50 Million Active Users forFreemium to Actually Work", SaaStr, September 2, 2012, https://www.SaaStr.com/you-need-50-million-users-for-freemium-to-actually-work/.
2. Lincoln Murphy, "There are 7 Types of Freemium and why that maters", Sixteen Ventures (blog), accessed October 2, 2017, http://sixteenventures.com/seven-types-of-freemium.
3. First Round Review, October 2017.
4. "Onboarding never stops", Inside Intercom (blog), September 19,2016, https://medium.com/intercom-inside/onboarding-never-stops-a9ccfd782ffd.
5. Brandall, Benjamin, "The Most Overlooked Aspect of UX Design Could Be the Most Important", TechCrunch, November 22, 2015, https://techcrunch.com/2015/11/22/the-most-overlooked-aspect-of-ux-design-could-be-the-most-important/.
6. Young, Nancy, "40 Clever Empty State Designs for Mobile Apps", Hongkiat, accessed October 2,2017, http://www.hongkiat.com/blog/mobile-app-empty-state-designs/.
7. "Onboarding checklist", Asana, accessed October 2, 2017, https://asana.com/guide/resources/checklists/onboarding-checklist.
8. Bill Zing, "Why Millennials Want Independence in Customer Support" Zingtree (blog), March 1, 2017, http://blog.zingtree.com/why-millennials-want-independence-in-customer-support/.

Chapter 11

1. Nguyen, Tien Anh, "Segmentation: A Guide to the Best B2B Practices", Openview, September 1, 2016, http://labs.openviewpartners.com/customer-segmentation/#.WaB0TXeGNp9.
2. BJ Fogg, "What Causes Behavior Change?", BJ Fogg's Behavior Model (blog), accessed October 2, 1017, http://www.behaviormodel.org/.

3. Greenburg, Guy, "The metrics that matter for successful gaming companies", Venture Beat, August 5, 2017, https://venturebeat.com/2017/08/05/the-metrics-that-matter-for-successful-gaming-companies/.

4. Hunter, Chay, "10 Monetization Tips for Mobile Games in 2017", Game Analytics, accessed October 2, 2017, http://www.gameanalytics.com/blog/monetization-tips-mobile-games-2017.html.

5. O'Donnell, Christopher, Pedro Magriço, and Brian Lafayette, Product-Led Growth Playbook (Boston: Openview, 2017), http://offers.openviewpartners.com/product-led-growth-playbook.

6. Patel, Sujan, "How to Write and Send Super Effective Re-Engagement Emails", Vero, February 18, 2015, https://www.getvero.com/resources/re-engagement-emails/.

7. Peet, James Gadsby, "Using Experimentation to Drive Product—Stephen Pavlovich (CEO of Conversion.com)", Mind the Product, March 20, 2017, https://www.mindtheproduct.com/2017/03/using-experimentation-drive-product/.

Chapter 12

1. Gnanasambandam, Chandra, et al, "Product managers for the digital world", McKinsey Quarterly, May 2017, http://www.mckinsey.com/industries/high-tech/our-insights/product-managers-for-the-digital-world.

2. Gothelf, Jeff, and Josh Seiden, Sense & Respond: How Successful Organizations Listen to Customers and Create New Products Continuously (Brighton Watertown: Harvard Business Review Press, 2017. http://senseandrespond.co/.

Chapter 13

1. Tomasz Tunguz, "Why Negative Churn is Such a Powerful Growth Mechanism", Tomasz Tunguz (blog), November 18, 2014, http://tomtunguz.com/negative-churn/.

2. David Skok, "SaaS Metrics 2.0—A Guide to Measuring and Improving What Matters", For Entrepreneurs (blog), accessed October 2, 2017, http://www.forentrepreneurs.com/SaaS-metrics-2/.

3. Tomasz Tunguz, "Fighting and Leveraging Inertia in Sales", Tomasz Tunguz (blog), August 4, 2016, http://tomtunguz.com/activation-energy-switching-costs/.

4. "5 Reasons Why Survey Respondents Don't Tell the Truth", Infosurv Research, Infosurv (blog), March 17, 2016, http://www.infosurv.com/5-reasons-why-survey-respondents-dont-tell-the-truth/.

5. Lemkin, Jason, "I Was Wrong. NPS is a Great Core Metric.", SaaStr, March 29, 2016, https://www.SaaStr.com/i-was-wrong-nps-is-a-great-core-metric/.

6. "How to Calculate LifetimeValue—The Infographic", Kissmetrics (blog), accessed October 2, 2017, https://blog.kissmetrics.com/how-to-calculate-lifetime-value/.

7. Ortwein, Eckhard, "Lean SaaS Metrics—The Definitive Guide to Create Business Impact", Move to SaaS, May 1, 2017, http://movetoSaaS.com/lean-SaaS-metrics-definitive-guide-create-business-impact/.

8. David Skok, "Startup Killer: The Cost of CustomerAcquisition", For Entrepreneurs (blog), accessed October 2, 2017, http://www.forentrepreneurs.com/startup-killer/.

9. Tunguz, Tomasz, "The Math Behind SaaS Startup Customer Lifetime Value", TechCrunch, August 28, 2015, https://techcrunch.com/2015/08/28/the-math-behind-SaaS-startup-valuation/.

10. Schrage, Michael, What Do You Want Your Customers to Become? (Brighton Watertown: Harvard Business Review Press, 2012), https://hbr.org/product/who-do-you-want-your-customers-to-become/11245-KND-ENG.

11. Schrage, Michael, "What Most Companies Miss About Customer Lifetime Value", Harvard Business Review, April 18, 2017, https://hbr.org/2017/04/what-most-companies-miss-about-customer-lifetime-value.

Chapter 14
1. Burt, Chris, "Slack May Be Sexier, But Office 365 Most Used Cloud-Based Business App", The Whir, March 29, 2016, http://www.thewhir.com/web-hosting-news/slack-may-be-sexier-but-office-365-most-used-cloud-based-business-app.

Chapter 15
1. Intrinsic Point (blog), accessed October 2, 2017, https://intrinsicpoint.com/.

2. Intrinsic Point (blog), op. cit.

Glossary

Average Customer Life (ACL): The total time (in days) of a relationship between a customer and the company. It measures an average number of days (or months) between the day a prospect becomes a customer and when the customer churns (or cancels).

Average Selling Price (ASP): The amount of revenue per customer generated.

Break-even: A point when a company generates enough revenue from a customer to cover all the costs and expenses it took to acquire this customer.

Contextual Engagement: This happens when the right customer receives the right messages at the right time through the right channel.

Customer Acquisition Cost (CAC): The average amount that a company spends to acquire a single customer. CAC is the sum of all customer acquisition costs, including sales and marketing expenses (and salaries), divided by the number of customers acquired during the same period.

Customer Behavior Index (CBI): A metric (often normalized) that measures how engaged your prospects and customers are based on their in-product activity and usage.

Customer Churn Rate: A percentage of customers lost due to churn (cancellation or failure to renew). It is calculated by dividing the number of churned customers by the number of customers at the start of the period for which churn rate is calculated.

Customer Touchpoint (or Customer Interaction): A single moment when a prospect or customer comes in contact with your brand, company, people, product, or message through various channels and devices.

Customer Experience (CX): A customer's perception about a company, brand, or product, based on all touchpoints, interactions, and engagements.

Customer Experience Era: The third wave of SaaS, where customers now research, evaluate, select, and share experiences that feel more like consumer experiences, including multiple touchpoints and interactions.

Customer Experience Strategy: An ongoing process of assessing and managing customer experiences across the customer lifecycle.

Customer Journey: A series of all touchpoints a customer has with a company, brand, and product to reach a certain milestone.

Customer Lifecycle: A framework that describes the process a customer goes through when considering, buying, using, and advocating a product or service. There are four critical stages: acquisition, adoption, retention, and expansion.

Customer Lifetime Value (CLV): A prediction of the net profit attributable to the entire future relationship with a customer. It is the revenue generated from customers between the time the company reaches the break-even point with them and the end of the relationship with them.

Customer Onboarding: The process of getting a newly subscribed customer (or account) up and running effectively with your product, including training, account and team member setup and assistance with integrations. The goal here is to set up the customer to realize the full value of your product, thereby retaining customers while also expanding business within the account, or getting referrals from your happy customers.

Customer Satisfaction Metrics: Shows how engaged customers are, how much value they derive from your product, and whether they will recommend your solution to peers. Customer satisfaction reflects how a customer perceives the value and experience with your company, brand, and product. A few examples of metrics in this category include Net Promoter Score (NPS), Customer Behavior Index (CBI), and Customer Lifetime Value (CLV).

Days to Break-Even: Measures the average number of days it takes a customer to generate enough revenue to cover the CAC. In other words, it shows how quickly a company recovers its CAC.

Days from PQL to Customer: Measures the average number of days it takes a PQL to become a customer.

Days from Signup to Customer: Measures the average number of days it takes a prospect to become a customer.

Days from Signup to PQL: Measures the average number of days it takes a prospect to become a PQL.

Digital Transformation: The change associated with the application of digital technology to all aspects of human society.

Engagement Loop: A practice of using insightful in-product usage data, along with engagement tactics, to influence prospects and customers to re-engage with the product and experience more value.

Free Trial: A customer acquisition model that provides a partial or complete product to prospects free of charge for a limited time. Typically, a free trial runs for 14 or 30 days.

Freemium: A customer acquisition model that provides access to part of a software product to prospects free of charge, without a time limit. A freemium product does not limit the amount of time a prospect can access the software, but often limits users in some way such as through stripped-back features or allowed amount of usage.

Go-To-Market (GTM) Strategy: An action plan that describes repeatable and scalable processes for how a company acquires, retains, and grows customers.

In-Product Call To Action (CTA): This reveals prospects' buying intentions and helps to drive prospects to PQLs or conversion events.

Initial Value Unit: An engagement or set of engagements that advance the customer through a core use case.

Loyalty Loop: A continuous process of delivering substantial value and customer experience to keep customers using the product, adopting new features, increasing usage, and renewing.

Moment of Joy: The time when a prospect feels the value in the product. Similar to the Moment of Truth; especially popular in the gaming industry. Successful product-led conversion connects moments of joy with recognition and rewards when a user performs a desired action.

Moment of Truth (MOT): In marketing, the moment when a customer/user interacts with a brand, product, or service in a way that serves to form or change an impression about that brand, product, or service.

MRR Churn Rate (a.k.a. Gross Revenue Churn): A percentage of MRR (Monthly Recurring Revenue) lost from existing customers at the start of the period for which MRR churn is calculated. MRR churn rate is always positive (positive churn rate means the company loses money), because it does not include upsell and cross-sell.

MRR Expansion Rate (a.k.a. Net Revenue Retention Rate): The percentage of MRR that is gained due to upsells and cross-sells to existing customers for the period for which MRR expansion is calculated. It is calculated by dividing the amount of expansion MRR by the starting MRR.

Net MRR Churn (a.k.a. Net Revenue Churn): The percentage of MRR change based on churned and expansion MRR for the same period. It is calculated by subtracting expansion MRR from churned MRR and dividing that by MRR at the start of the period. Net MRR churn is the percentage of MRR lost from existing customers in a period.

Non-Product Engagements: All of the interactions that prospects have outside of your product. See "Product Engagements."

Omnichannel Approach: Companies create contextual engagements with customers that look and feel the same across channels and devices.

Personalized Customer Experience: An ongoing process of designing and delivering targeted messages and experiences that create meaningful customer engagements.

PQL-To-Customer Rate: The percentage of PQLs that convert to customers. It is calculated by dividing the number of customers by the number of PQLs. The PQL-to-customer rate shows how effectively your company converts PQLs to customers.

Product Champion: The person who has the highest level of engagement with your product, and has a good understanding of who will be using your product in his/her organization, as well as which roles each user has.

Product Engagements: All of the interactions that prospects have inside of your product. See "Non-product engagements."

Product-Led Go-To-Market Strategy: An action plan that describes repeatable and scalable processes for how a company acquires, retains, and grows customers, driven by in-product customer behavior, feedback, product usage, and analytics.

Product Lifecycle: A framework that helps a company organize its marketing and sales of a product, from introducing it to the market to when sales peak and decline.

Product/Market Fit: An experimentation process of finding customers in a target market with a problem that your product can address for a price (or total cost of ownership) well below the level of value that's provided in exchange. A broader but related concept, company/market fit, combines pain-product fit and customer-message fit ideas.

Product-Qualified Lead (PQL): A prospect that signed up and demonstrated buying intent based on product interest, usage, and behavioral data.

Prospect (or User) Onboarding: How a prospect moves through initial signup, experiences initial value, and reaches PQL status. It is designed to help users become familiar with the product and realize initial value as soon as possible.

Signup-to-Customer Rate: The percentage of signups that become paying customers. It is calculated by dividing the number of customers by the number of signups. The signup-to-customer rate shows how your company, on average, converts signups to customers.

Signup-to-PQL Rate: The percentage of prospects that complete profile and in-product engagement requirements to become product qualified leads (PQLs). It is calculated by dividing the number of PQLs by the number of signups. The signup-to-PQL rate provides insights into how effectively your company engages prospects in the early stages of reaching initial value.

Note: In some cases, it makes sense to analyze signup-to-PQL rate in terms of individual and account signups.

Unified Customer Profile Data: Your organization's system of record for all customer profile, company, and behavioral data.

Value Gap: The discrepancy between what a customer expects from the product and the value received or perceived.

Value-Based Pricing: This involves knowing which product features customers value most.

Valued (Golden) Features: These help companies understand which product capabilities deliver customer value and fill the Value Gap. The idea also provides a mechanism to know which customers receive value from product features, and which customers are not engaged at key stages in their lifecycle.

Velocity Metrics: Describes how long it takes a company to achieve certain milestones. This includes the average number of days it takes a prospect to go from signup to becoming a PQL, and the average number of months it takes a company to break even (when CLV>CAC).

Visitor-to-Signup Rate: The percentage of visitors that visit your page and then sign up. It is calculated by dividing the number of product signups by the number of visitors to a signup page. The visitor-to-signup rate shows how effectively your company convinces visitors to sign up for free trials or a freemium.

Zero Data (Empty State): What a prospect sees during their initial signup process when no data is available in the product. To address this, guide the prospect through a journey that populates, uploads, or integrates data to a product.

About the Authors

Nick Bonfiglio

Nick Bonfiglio is a 25-year industry veteran and one of the early Internet Software as a Service champions. He is currently CEO and cofounder of Aptrinsic, a SaaS company providing a personalized product experience platform that is transforming how companies build and monetize software. Most recently, Nick spent seven years at Marketo, where, as EVP of Global Product, he was responsible for all product management, engineering, operations and technical support. At Marketo, he focused on building the product and the next-generation platform, and reimagining user interfaces for the future.

TWITTER: twitter.com/Nick_Bonfiglio LINKEDIN: www.linkedin.com/in/nickbonfiglio
MEDIUM: medium.com/@nick_99633 QUORA: www.quora.com/profile/Nick-Bonfiglio-2

Mickey Alon

Mickey Alon is a 17-year industry veteran with significant software development and engineering experience. He is currently Chief Product Officer and cofounder of Aptrinsic, a SaaS company providing a personalized product experience platform that is transforming how companies build and monetize software. Most recently, Mickey was Group Vice President at Marketo, where he led global engineering and product management for web personalization and predictive content. He was also the CEO and cofounder of Insightera, which was acquired by Marketo in 2013.

TWITTER: twitter.com/mickey_alon LINKEDIN: www.linkedin.com/in/malon
MEDIUM: medium.com/@mickey.alon.21

About Aptrinsic

Aptrinsic provides a personalized product experience platform to help companies acquire, retain, and grow customers by creating real-time, personalized engagements driven by product usage. Your product is your best sales tool - we help unlock its potential.

TWITTER: twitter.com/aptrinsic
LINKEDIN: www.linkedin.com/company/12954370
BLOG - INTRINSIC POINT: intrinsicpoint.com